MODEL TO BUILD TRUST HO

JORGE FARÍAS ARIZPE

MODEL TO BUILD TRUST HO

©Jorge Farías Arizpe 2021. All rights reserved.

Proofreading and editing: Luis Gálvez.

Translator: Ismael Martínez Moreno

Cover design: Gabriela Vallín

Kindle Direct Publishing

ISBN: 9798780121978

Paperback edition 2021.

To all those people who embrace and practice the discipline of Trustability and above all, to all those devoted to teaching, and motivate the new generations in this discipline.

Trust touches the mind, heart, and soul. It suits everyone; it is the seed that naturally sprouts and builds consensus.

Be Trusted by others and you will be Happy; Being a person who is not trusted by others will make you unhappy.

Be a Trustworthy Provider of love, useful products and services to your neighbor, children, parents, partner, neighbors, friends, both casual and regular clients and you will reap blessings.

Whatever you do right and deliver with joy, blooms.

JORGE FARÍAS

INDEX

INTRODUCTION XIII

FOREWORD XXI

CHAPTER I CULTURE OF TRUSTABILITY 25
    1- DEFINITIONS OF BEING A TRUSTWORTHY PERSON 25
    2- ETHICAL CAUSES OF TRUST 27
    3- A COMBINATION OF FUNDAMENTAL ELEMENTS TO BE TRUSTWORTHY 32
    4- ANTHROPOLOGICAL BASIS OF THE TRUSTWORTHY PERSON 35
    5- TRUST IN REAL LIFE 39
    6- WHO CAN YOU BE TRUSTED BY? 51
    7- WHEN IS TRUST LOST? 53
    8- ANTIDOTES TO LOW HUMAN TRUST 56
    9- WHAT IS REQUIRED TO ACHIEVE INSTITUTIONAL TRUST? 57

CHAPTER II MODEL TO BUILD TRUST HO 61
    SCHEMATIC SYNTHESIS OF THE MODEL TO BUILD TRUST HO 63
    II.1. MANAGEMENT COMMITMENT AND AWARENESS RAISING 67
    II.2. IMPLEMENTATION OF THE MODEL TO BUILD TRUST 69
    II.3. MANAGEMENT OF THE MODEL TO BUILD TRUST HO. 194
    II.4. CONFLICTS OF INTEREST 196
    II.5. COMPLEMENTARY EXPLANATIONS TO THE MODEL 202

CHAPTER III TRUST PURPOSES 217
    1- WELLBEING 217
    2- SELF-ESTEEM AND WELLBEING 219
    3- THE WELLBEING OF OTHERS 220
    4- WELLBEING - TRUST BINOMIAL 221
    5- WELLBEING - USE BINOMIAL 223
    6- USE-QUALITY BINOMIAL IN THE STRUCTURE OF THE GOOD 224
    7- USE-QUALITY BINOMIAL IN THE MANUFACTURING PROCESSES OF THE PRODUCT 224
    8- WELLBEING - TRUST 225

EPILOGUE **WELL-BEING, HAPPINESS AND FULFILLMENT** *235*
  1- WHY DID YOU COME INTO THE WORLD? 235
  2- TRUST PATH 236
  3- WELLBEING 238
  4- HAPPINESS 238
  5- PLENITUDE 239

BIBLIOGRAPHY *241*

JORGE FARIAS ARIZPE *243*

INTRODUCTION

MY BASIC CULTURE

During my studies of the Japanese Model, in the Total Quality disciplines, in Management, back in the eighties, working for CYDSA and later, when I visited Japan, something that left a strong impact on me was the Trustability of the people, systems, methods and processes they manage, with the Quality approach and the results that this has on the performance (successful performance) both of the society and of the country.

At CYDSA, where I worked for 20 years, we were able to implement a Quality culture with many people convinced of the *Quality Model*, with extraordinary results in terms of efficiency, profitability, client satisfaction, provider compliance and work environment.

There is a high correlation between a well-functioning country and its *Quality Model*. Likewise, there is a high correlation with a poorly or mediocrely performing country when there is a lack of or a clear contradiction with what the Quality Model says. The Model I am referring to may be explicit or implicit in the country's culture.

I learned that many people from all educational levels have the potential and the seed to be trustworthy people, as long as they are surrounded by a quality environment, starting with their superiors, and continuing with a Quality Culture of human, personal and organizational trustworthiness.

I realized that there is a correlation between some of the principles of the Quality Model and some of what I learned from the Marist Brothers in Christian/Catholic religion classes in elementary school and from my parents, which was the following: *Never tell lies because God is watching you and you can't hide, no matter how much you want to.*

Better the truth. Better to be Transparent. In the long run, everything will come out.

In the *Quality Model* it is called Transparency with documentation and objectivity, that is: knowing how to identify *what it is*, which is different from *what you want it to be* (note: the Japanese are neither Catholic nor Christian, only a minority, but they act on the basis of an inherited tradition, which is Buddhist).

In various religions it is called: Truth and Congruence, which will make you truly happy and free.

Also, there are already video cameras in cities (stores, offices, public places, among others), so it is technically possible for you to be observed. I know of some cases where they are already trying to videotape the whole life of a human being, from birth to death. Today technology makes it possible, and I remember what I was taught as a child: you can't hide, even if you want to.

Imagine how people would be and act if they were videotaped every moment of their lives and were asked to back up and verify what they said.

I am an engineer, and in classes, I studied about trust in electromechanical devices. I learned to classify them according to their Trustworthiness: if they fail, they are not

Trustworthy. I learned which cycle was more likely to fail and under what circumstances. Thus I was able to classify and observe expected results according to Trust. Whenever I can, I apply these learnings to myself, and then to the people I observe.

The year 2005 was a watershed of events that marked my life: the Year 2005 was a watershed of events that impacted my life: in early January, I suffered a severe spinal injury; my beloved mother passed away on January 28 and my father in May; in August, I made an unforgettable trip with Paty, my daughter; in October, I was blessed by meeting María Esther, my wife, who, by the way, sent me a book by David Hawkins, before we met; and so I had the fortune to read Hawkins, in his book, *Power versus Force*. Here I found yet another element that aims, indisputably, at the topic and the objective of being a Quality, Trustworthy Person, with a focus on Truth, on Objectivity.

David Hawkins says that, in the cell system, the body responds with health to Truth and Congruence, while it responds with disease to lies. After reading Hawkins, I found several health authors, such as the prestigious Louise Hay, who corroborate that most diseases can be foreseen, and that they are caused by emotional aspects linked to negative feelings. Throughout my life, I have witnessed both perceptions: both what happens with the practice of Truth and Congruence and what happens with the other extreme: lying on purpose.

Personally, I have specialized in Emotional Intelligence: there it is shown, in a very evident way, that Truth and Congruence are communicated in different ways and are perceived by people who are sensitive, and it is a key element for the emotion proficiency.

HIGHLIGHTS IN MY TRUSTWORTHINESS STORY

- Japanese *Quality Model*.
- Religious principle of not lying.
- Trust engineering.
- The human capacity to learn the *Quality Model*.
- Video cameras watching you.
- According to Hawkins, our body reveals the truth and the lie: the lie that produces tension, disease and division, the truth that brings looseness, unification, and balance.
- Emotional Intelligence.

And in the end, all in all, there is a common element in all of these approaches: TRUTH and OBJECTIVITY are the keys to a healthy life and not only healthy, but also efficient, with good results, being useful to others.

PURPOSE OF THE BOOK

This book is a sequel to the previous book entitled: El Reto de México: Aumentar la Confiabilidad.

The purpose is to teach the concepts to be applied in companies and organizations on the *know-how* to increase Trustability, and to show the Technical Model of Factors to be implemented to ensure Trustability.

I believe that this model is applicable to all countries and individuals who wish to structure an institutional trustworthiness assurance system.

I am convinced that Trustability is for the benefit of each of the people who practice this discipline, and that it automatically extends to their families, companies, and institutions. In the same way, it promotes social structuring for the benefit of a whole country and the world.

BE MORE TRUSTWORTHY TO OTHERS.

IT IS CONVENIENT FOR US.

FOREWORD

The intention I have in this book is to generate a specialty of TRUSTABILITY in our environment, so that we can develop experts in Trustability to help companies, institutions, and families to practice this beautiful art or sport for the common benefit.

Given the complexity of the products and services we consume, we need to be especially committed to make sure that they are trustworthy from all points of view.

1. The point of view of its Use and its attachment, adaptation to the use given to that product or service.

    There is a difference between a car for the highway and a car for narrow streets, for winding roads, for loading material or for passengers.

    This is how it is with every product we purchase and then customize for our needs. With Trustability awareness and expert help in Trustability, we will make a proper, efficient, and safe use, and therefore, satisfactory, in feeling that customization of the product or service.

2. Is the point of view of your structure built to last, to endure, to withstand rough use or is it made to serve temporarily?

    Big difference. Of course, it depends on its use. Therefore, first of all, it is necessary to deepen in this specialty of TRUSTABILITY, in the use it will have, in order to then judge its structure.

3. The point of view of its Design in terms of aesthetics. Again, it depends on its use, but in particular, on who it is aimed at and the taste patterns, fashion, and habits of those who will use that product or service.

   It is important to note that service is increasingly linked to the product. Increasingly, the product involves service, from the way it is delivered, to the way it is provided and maintained, to the way it is withdrawn from use. And in the future, it looks like there will be more and more product and service customization.

   Customization means, naturally, a technically supported democratization, with many providers working on the service to others.

4. From the point of view of the Processes used to elaborate the product or service, are they robust, efficient processes to lower the cost and price for the clients? Are the processes trustworthy in terms of ensuring that there is quality control to avoid defects and failures? Are they executed by well-trained and qualified people who are recognized for their good performance?

5. From People's point of view, there is a big difference between people working on the spur of the moment and people who are focused, committed and have a vocation for what they do. This is the so-called human side of the company, of the business.

6. The point of view in the Information Technologies, the automated, digitalized systems, at the service of the client and the user. Personalization of needs, tastes

and desires is now possible, thanks to this enormous capacity to handle massive data and information on clients and choice alternatives.

Personalization can only be achieved with the ability to handle data and information that digitized, and electronically operated information technology has.

The results are not automatic, because I say so and I want it that way, but the results come from a team of people with wills and talents that determine whether the result is of high level of Trustability, medium level or poor level of Trustability in terms of the six points of view mentioned in this prologue: *Use, Structure, Design, Processes, People,* and *Information Technology.*

In this book you will be able to observe and assimilate ideas for your own development of Trustability and also to apply it to companies, organizations, and institutions, where a group of people work collaboratively and aligned to a Trusted client service.

CHAPTER I
CULTURE OF TRUSTABILITY

1- DEFINITIONS OF BEING A TRUSTWORTHY PERSON

Trusted comes from trustworthy, THAT INSPIRES CONFIDENCE, SECURITY, WORTHY OF FAITH AND CREDIBILITY.

A trusted person is someone who provides security, offers guarantees or is dependable in their actions and in their speech.

This refers to the impact of oneself on others. To be perceived as a dependable or reliable person: trustworthy.

Could you be trustworthy if you tell everything the other person likes to hear, or could you only be trustworthy if you speak truthfully and objectively, not out of personal convenience to gain some advantage in return for yourself?

Is it because the trustworthy person has fundamental rules to follow, knows them, follows them and that's enough, or is it because, without rules, they act in good faith, impartially and wisely, making the right recommendations and deciding successfully, demonstrating that their decisions have yielded good results?

The answer is that to be trustworthy and credible, you have to perform well in both cases, following good rules; or when there are no rules, or they are not good, decide wisely, without them.

It is practically impossible to do so in all fields of knowledge and in all specialties of the world.

For this reason, Trustability is almost always recognized as referring to a field of knowledge, a field of play, a specialty, a trade. There are exceptionally trustable people in many fields or trades.

3 Types of human relationships:
1. Family relationship in parent/child matters: family.
2. Relationship between adults with no commitment to share goods or tasks.
3. Relationship between adults exchanging resources, tasks, goods.

The Model to Build Trust will focus more on Type 3 Human Relationship, between adults.

Speaking of material elements, equipment, machines, or tools, it is important to define their Trustability and, according to the Royal Spanish Academy, Trustability is simply that something works well. This essence refers, mainly, to the High Probability of Good Performance part of the equation, to which I will refer next.

HIGH PROBABILITY OF GOOD PERFORMANCE.

Imagine how important it is for an aircraft to be Reliable. Lives are at stake. Low Trustability leads to human fatalities. The pilot must be very trustable.

Much more so the Presidency of a country, the Minister of Defense, the Minister of Finance, the General Director of food companies, transportation companies, etc.

In the world of people who play a role, an activity that has results, we can say, if the person works well in their role, it is very likely that their place where they work, their organization, institution, or company where they are, is also Trustworthy. The more authority that person has, the more impact they have on your organization. Good performance generally means good Trustability.

When companies, organizations and businesses are performing efficiently, it is because their people are adequately competent in the job they perform.

2- ETHICAL CAUSES OF TRUST

PERSONAL MOTIVATION FOR TRUTH

There is an inner chip, as David Hawkins says, which is found in our human nature, where the connection between our cells lies, which, when they are connected and are part of our muscles and organs, then, they realize when there are inconsistencies between our intention, our beliefs, our words, our decisions, actions and, when there are clear inconsistencies between what is said and what is done, there is a clear, internal alert of imbalance, which is noticed muscularly, cellularly, organically, which can be measured with detection of electrical impulses and *micro-perceived* muscular tension and, above all, which is noticed at the level of attitudes, fears, motivations and body behavior of the person.

So, truth is not something that can be modulated on a whim, it is not something intangible that remains on the margin of the tangible, but it is an intangible that becomes something evident and noticeable to others and to yourself, if you focus on it, if you concentrate on this process and on your inner self. The others, sooner or later, realize it.

That intangible, which is transformed into something tangible, is when from a thought and an intention (intangible), a hormone is produced, which is a chemical substance (tangible) and travels throughout your body through your blood and all your cells. In addition, there are electrical impulses that run through your nervous system. For example: when you have one type of thought, the substance called DOPAMINE is produced, but if you have a different type of thought and intention, you produce a very different substance known as SEROTONIN. More importantly, dopamine produces very different and sometimes opposite effects to the effects produced by serotonin. In other words, your body notices the difference. Dopamine can negatively affect your cells, and serotonin acts positively. One possible consequence is discomfort while another one may be energizing. In addition, accumulation matters. I mean that accumulated discomfort becomes disease; accumulated well-being becomes health.

Hawkins' thesis, and that of many scholars of human behavior, is: *if you relapse into lying, sooner or later the imbalance caused makes you sick and it is cumulative*, like not sleeping at ease, it is a symptom of an inner malaise.

Therefore, under this conception, under this perspective, being a *gandalla*[1] sooner or later hurts or makes you sick.

With all these realities of internal cellular connections, which detect the truth, or the lie and the incongruity, there is still the game of individual preferences and will, where each person bets on the truth, every moment, every event.

There are 2 Levels of personal action in relation to truth:

1. Truth motivation, that is, the voluntary search for truth, for the pleasure and challenge of its content and the attractiveness of the objective curiosity, that is, to discover more and more or, on the contrary, to confirm formulated hypotheses.

2. The motivation for personal gain (gandalla), referring to those who ignore or underestimate the truth and internal cellular connections to come out with a narrative different from the truth; that is, with and incomplete truth that favors personal interests and provides the pride of a momentary satisfaction, for the ability to achieve personal gain or personal taste.

Level 1 promotes Trustability while Level 2 promotes Untrustability.

At Level 1, you may perceive that your desire is one, but reality is another. One thing is *what you see*; another is *what*

---

[1] One who is abusive and has bad intentions.

others see; and another, different, is what *reality may be*. That is the search for truth and consensus.

At Level 2, your desire is one and *what you see*, which *is reality*, is *that very thing*. What you want to see, is the same as what, according to you, is reality, and it is not. You confuse reality with *what you want it to be*.

Honesty is the human quality that is most appreciative of and most attached to the truth.

THE NEIGHBOR'S PERSPECTIVE

Trustworthy is a person's perspective on their fellow man, what other people are to them.

This cause is an internal belief that conditions the attitudes you have towards yourself and others. First, it is the deep belief and from there, as a consequence, the attitudes follow, then the decisions and your actions.

The untrustworthy person is convinced that others must be trustworthy towards them, not themselves towards others, why?

Because they perceive them as subjects, as servants, as inferiors, that is what they reflect when they want to impose, when they want them to be unconditional, with blind obedience. They make it clear that, for them, others are inferior, they must obey them, be loyal and trustworthy because they have certain power over them.

If they perceive others as adversaries or enemies to be controlled, minimized, or eliminated, they cause the effect of being untrustworthy (at least with those they qualify as enemies).

It turns out that, with this perspective of the neighbor, seen as a subject or adversary, one automatically sees *the speck in the other's eye and does not see the log in one's own*. You cannot be Trustworthy to others when you criticize them, while you do the same or worse.

The automatic consequence of this perspective is that they ARE NOT RELIABLE. If they act on this premise, the results of human interaction cannot be healthy, tolerable, or sustainable.

The evidence of not being Trustworthy is betrayal of the other.

If for you, others are your servants or adversaries, you are not Trustworthy.

If you see them as enemies or adversaries, you will think that what they tell you is not true, and you will not act truthfully with them either.

If you see them as subjects, you have more rights than they do, and they have no reason to complain.

If you see them as inferior, you decide what to do and what not to do, because they are not at your level of judgment and if they were to decide, they would be wrong.

In conclusion, you don't trust them, and you want them to trust you. It is a contradiction that human nature will take care to disprove, because your perspective of your fellow man is a falsehood. Human nature is very wise and will end up, sooner or later, disproving you for your serious error of perception, of perspective, and it will not be by the kind way, but by the way of strongly felt consequences.

It is not a matter of ideology. Hitler and Stalin, with opposite ideologies, reached the same goal: the destruction of others, first their fellow man, then their self-destruction. Both characters die violent and controversial deaths. With their thoughts and desires, they die in conditions of hardship and stress, after having caused the death of so many people.

3- A COMBINATION OF FUNDAMENTAL ELEMENTS TO BE TRUSTWORTHY

According to field of activity:

1. Being Ethical.
2. Be Competent.

According to the relationship with others:

1. To know and feel the truth, (or whatever comes closest to the truth) and act in accordance with it.
2. To treat others with that truth (not only knowledge of things, but knowledge of people; that is, to know and feel the emotional part of people). Be Trustworthy to them. Do not betray.

According to personal inner qualities:

1. Be fair.
2. To have wisdom.

In other words:

1. Do not be selfish.
2. Not to be ignorant.

In the perspective of the other:

1. To be trustworthy is to never betray them.

2. To be trustworthy is to be credible, to support you based on what you can and do honestly and ethically.

When your fellow man depends on you (children, spouse, workers in your service, family members) Trustability takes on another meaning, which is to NOT FAIL THEM. Many times it is placing their wellbeing above your own.

To clarify, it is not that easy. It is not enough to be good in the goodness dimension, nor is it enough to be good in the competence dimension, in your field. In addition, you need to be credible, which depends on third parties and not only on yourself. How do others perceive you? To be, and to make the other feel that you are trustworthy. For that, you first need to trust you, that you are Trustworthy. Your conviction shows in your body language.

In other words, a trustworthy person earns the adjective trustworthy when they move within the framework of being honorable and ethical; that is, they handle themselves with the truth and, in addition, are competent in the matter in question, because they are an experienced person, prepared to face and come out well from the adversity that their profession presents and, in addition, if they also achieve exceptional results that are presented in non-typical cases.

Trustability chain has 4 elements, which are: Ethics, Intelligence, Continuous preparation, many hours of flight in the field or subject in question, with good results, starting from Beginner; then, Intermediate; then, Advanced; and finally, Expert and Master. Intelligence, continuous preparation, and many hours of flight, generate a competence or a sum of competences of an activity or a trade.

There are societies and cultures that highly stimulate these 4 Elements and become successful. On the contrary, there are communities or cultures that despise these elements of the chain and society becomes a disgrace.

To be trustworthy, in a complete way, it is required to have character to be able to walk that path of combining Ethics, Intelligence, Preparation and many hours of flight, with good performance in the trade or activity that is practiced. It also means having the patience and endurance; that is: the Emotional Intelligence to start from Beginner, move on to Intermediate, Advanced, Expert and Master. In addition to character, vocation is required. Now it has been said to have passion as well. Well, if you are on the right path and turn on the speed that passion gives you, it is very commendable, but beware of blindly ignoring passion, because sometimes, it unbalances you and takes you away from the trustworthy and safe path.

He who is honest, does not undertake to do what he does not know how to do, or he does it by clearly manifesting to others its scope, he does not give an opinion on what he does not know, or, if he does not know for sure, he formulates a hypothesis subject to be tested and so he manifests it.

He who is honest, necessarily, investigates when he does not know and it is something that concerns him and, above all, for which he is responsible.

Ignorance is the cause of many Trustability failures. There are many people who think they are honest because they do not steal, but they reject science, research and testing and, at bottom, it can be said that these people are not honest.

HONESTY AND COMPETENCE ARE INDISPENSABLE FOR ACHIEVING TRUST

Dishonesty is a sufficient cause of untrustability; the dishonest is always untrustable.

Regarding the Competence element, the key components are: Rational Intelligence applied in the trade, Preparation; Flight Hours in the trade and Good performance; in order to develop them, it requires character formation to transform oneself, facing adversity.

Character, Vocation, and the 4 Elements of the Trustability chain (Ethics, Intelligence applied to your craft, Preparation and Flight Hours), are key to producing High Trustability. In this chapter, we will examine these human factors in more detail.

Chemically speaking, when two substances are mixed in a suitable proportion, the result is a compound that gives rise to a third substance, with unique properties different from those of the original substances. Example: mix oxygen and hydrogen in a certain proportion and you get water, which by itself is an immensely useful substance. This is how Trustability should be seen: the substance HONESTY is humanly combined with the substance COMPETENCE and generates a third substance: TRUST, which in itself has consistency and structure, can be managed, measured, and developed. This is how we will approach Trustability in this book.

4- ANTHROPOLOGICAL BASIS OF THE TRUSTWORTHY PERSON

1. (+) Life must prevail over death (+);

but:

2. (-) Hunger and poverty produce death (-);

however:

3. (+) Food and health give you life, solve the problem of death (+);

however:

4. Food and health cost and require remuneration or economic wealth, starting with having enough to eat;

then:

5. (+) Remuneration and economic assets should be used for health and to solve the problem of hunger and poverty (+);

but you could misuse them:

6. (-) Remuneration and economic assets, you could use them for apparently human satisfactions, contrary to health and produce illness or early death (-);

and you have 2 options:

6.1. (+) Remuneration and economic assets are obtained by lawful work (+);

6.2. (+) Remuneration and economic assets are obtained by lawful work (+).

Any animal instinctively masters Factor 1, knows about Factor 2, intuitively masters Factor 3, and masters Factor 4 and 5. With those 5 Factors, it automatically looks for food to subsist, but the last Factor, it can no longer even consider. The human does. The animal is not trustworthy, nor honorable, it is automatic and unconscious. Humans are either Trustworthy or Untrustworthy. Humans have a will and a character that animals do not have, to discern the end and the means, in the light of a more complex and elevated society.

To be a Trustworthy person, you need to achieve the chain of the 4 Factors in positive (+).

The first Factor in the above list, becomes the end of Trustability, which is life over death, wellbeing, and progress (that wellbeing be as sustainable as possible).

I mean that, in order to be a Trustworthy person, you need to be compatible with a Life Purpose (your END), Factor 1, but it is not enough, you also need to use the right means to reach that end (your HOW), the next 3 Factors. This process identifies you and others notice it.

It is not free, Trustability requires effort, a fight against inertia and against comfort.

Positive (+) thoughts belong to life-oriented thoughts.

The lawful work (6.1 in positive) necessarily produces a service to others, to the common good, since the remuneration you get comes from a disbursement made by others to you, for some service you provided to someone.

This is the basic chain to produce Trustability. To this chain, we will add, consecutively, links to ensure Trustability with other complementary elements of the *Quality Model*, in order to have a *Model to Build Trust*.

To be Trusted by others, you need to demonstrate consistency, i.e., show many times that your decisions and actions are Trustworthy.

Always lawful work, remuneration and assets well spent and well invested systematically, having good results at all times and, when not, always correcting, growing in talent and responsibility.

The mistakes must be handled in an objective manner and in the struggle for human correctness. No one is obliged to do what is impossible, but the person who is Trustworthy will always be willing to correct, when necessary, in order to continue to get it right in the future and avoid substantial failures or mistakes.

The Trustworthy person identifies faults and corrects them. Knows objectively that order and Trustworthiness, costs.

Later, in the *Model to Build Trust*, we will see that there are incidental failures and accidental failures. The incidental ones do not end in an accident, because they precede and predict the accident, but it does not occur.

Trustability is gained after a long time, after a continuous struggle, after many successes that generate a trend, however, Trustability can be lost very quickly, with one or several accidents.

You cannot be a Trustworthy person if you incur in any of the factors in negative (-). And less Trustworthy, you are if they are recurrent or continuous.

Trustability has to do with the ends you pursue, they must be Trustworthy, but it is not enough, the means you use must also be Trustworthy. In *Chapter III,* we will see the *Aims of Trustability*.

HIGHLIGHTS TO REMEMBER:
- Pursue sustainable life and well-being.
- Health, in order to preserve life, costs.
- Remuneration and economic wealth are not an absolute guarantee to achieve health, it depends on how you use them.

- Therefore, Remuneration and economic assets are not a guarantee of giving you Trustability.
- The chain to produce death or disease is very easy to perform, it is naturally attractive, that is, with any carelessness you have, you fall into one of the 3 Factors in negative (-).
- To be a Trustworthy Person, you need to link the 4 Factors in positive (+) and avoid the negative (-), which implies that you are very capable, both in your honesty and in your competence.

5- TRUST IN REAL LIFE

FIELDS OF ACTION AND DECISION

Real life presents different Fields of Specialization. It is impossible for a person, during their lifetime, to master all the fields that our world has to offer. Some of these fields are humanity, animals, plants, earth, mountains, oceans, firmament, stars, material things, equipment, tools, houses, and other goods that have been created with science and technology.

The people, universities, science, technology, and associations dedicated to these fields have been documenting and classifying the different specialties and subjects of knowledge and have left a written memory of this knowledge.

There are not only fields of knowledge that are studied in universities and sciences. There are fields of expertise in the arts, sports, crafts, trades, and craftsmanship in the world of life in general, in the world of entertainment and amusement, that demand to be trusted. The job of being a parent, being a citizen or being a housewife, are of fundamental importance in life and require trustworthy people to perform them. Here again it applies that, to be Trustworthy, the binomial is required: Ethics and Competence in the Trade. It is a challenge to be trustable.

In all these innumerable trades, there are incorrect practices due to ethical or competence faults, and there are also different degrees of correct performance in Trustability, according to the ethical capacities and skills and competence capabilities. In all these countless trades, there is no ceiling as to say: *There is no better way to do it*, but you can always do it better. Total perfection is very difficult and can only be reached in a certain finite time, according to certain pre-established rules, because with time, everything changes, everything is dynamic and, as circumstances change, so do the ways of executing the trades. It is like the performance of a dance, a concert, a sports game, a product, or a service.

There are 2 Layers of Depth in managing diagnoses, solutions, and decisions in each of these myriad trades:

1. A more superficial layer is where the domain is by common sense and brief explanation and exposition (Common Field of Action: CFA), where every adult person can act without requiring specialization or certification of their skills and knowledge. Generally, the consequences of not knowing, in this case, only affect oneself or one's very close circle. They belong to the family world.

2. Deeper layer of issues, problems with more complexity, which demand a specialized domain (Specialized Field of Action: SFA), which requires a capacity, preparation, involvement in a specialization

of life and its nature that not everyone masters, which requires dedicating time for study and deepening, having intelligence and dedication.

An example that distinguishes these 2 Layers is deciding what to eat: Egg, beans, pork rinds or everything; being healthy, that decision is a CFA. But decide what to eat, egg, beans, or both, while sick with severe intestinal infection, becomes SFA.

Choosing where to sit inside a commercial aircraft is CFA; but sitting in the pilot's seat and operating the aircraft is SFA. Flying as a passenger requires a certain capacity (CFA) but flying as a pilot requires a very different one (SFA).

So, speaking of Being a Trustworthy Person, it is very important to separate these 2 Layers of different depths, as clearly as possible and say, first, to yourself:

1. Do I master the subject or not? Is it CFA or SFA?
2. Is the decision only for me and only I am affected, or are other people, besides me, affected?
3. Are the consequences of the decision to be made serious or trivial?

Honestly answering these 3 questions, is how you begin to weave the first links in the chain that produces Trustability and, by letting others know, they are the ones who determine the degree of your Credibility, they Believe and Trust you, or they do not.

What it really is, *what you think it is, what others think it is,* and based on that, agree whether you are credible or not, according to others.

Let's delve, next, into How to Be More Trustworthy, in the World of Deeper Specialization: SFA. In the field where there are more doubts because it is a more complex field.

- What to do when there are people who know more than you do about the subject?
    - *Ask for their permission and collaboration so that you can learn.*
- What to do when we know more than others on the subject in question?
    - *Ask their permission by convincing them to use your diagnosis or your solution, as the case may be, and check them honestly and ethically.*
- What to do when we are all ignorant of the subject?
    - *Start from the truth and ask for time and resources to learn the truth.*

PHASES OF MASTERY, OR DEPTH, OR DEGREE OF SPECIALIZATION IN THE TRADE, WITHIN WHAT FALLS (SPECIALIZED FIELD OF ACTION)

In each of these countless Trades or Fields of Specialization, I find at least 4 major Phases to deepen them:

Phase 1: *Beginners*. The most common and general aspects of the Craft, with their corresponding rules and solution recipes.

First, to be competent in mastering the most known and studied structured Field, to know its basic rules, to be obedient and adherent to them, I mean to have rules with fundamentals, to respect and follow those correct and proven rules.

Have knowledge and experience in knowing the fundamentals (have basic competence: here are the beginners).

Phase 2: *Intermediate*. Generally, in all Crafts, there are major challenges that not everyone can execute, only a few can do it in the next Layer of depth or specialization, due to their inner gifts, to the skills they have developed, little by little, or to the skills they have achieved, through strong training.

Phase 3: *Advanced*. In this phase, a greater capacity for mastery, development and practice is consolidated, so that a more consistent execution can be achieved. Greater depth and diversity of solutions, with a greater number of weapons and resources available to meet the challenges of the trade. Generally, at this stage, it is already possible to start co-creating different and novel solutions that improve the knowledge and/or practice of the Trade.

Phase 4: *Experts and Masters*. In this Phase, great abilities and skills are combined with many hours of practice flight, with a good number of successful results and, in addition, adding new solutions, co-created by them, which enrich the Trade.

Of course, there may be subgrades within each phase, depending on the complexity of the job and the risks inherent in performing it. Beginners A, B and C, for example.

There is a great variety of jobs or applications for each trade, from those that present only very low risks, with little complexity to perform them, to those that present very high risks and a great deal of complexity to perform them. For example, driving a car entails very diverse risks; doing so in uninhabited and well-conditioned areas for driving practice entails low risk; on the other hand, driving on racetracks, in Formula 1 races, with very valuable and dangerous cars, or driving trucks with explosive material, entails high risk to one's own and other people's property.

The important thing now, in order to correctly manage your Trustability, is to make a *matching,* that is to say, a *conjugation*, a *comparison,* between your abilities and competences, and the competences required by the project or job in question, in terms of complexity and risk.

In other cases, to drive a passenger vehicle, you do not need the same skills as driving a Formula 1 car, but you do need the ethics and complete honesty, you do need to drive cars with driver certification/credentials to carry passengers. Therefore, Trustability must be measured in that work, in those circumstances in which the playing field was designed. Competencies appropriate to the job or project, ethics, and complete honesty, with the vision to measure results to make the history of Trustability, according to the facts.

The attitude you have in each phase of advancement is very important for your credibility. In other words, the perception that others have of your trustworthiness is your credibility in the eyes of others.

The ideal is to have the right attitude according to the stage you are in, in terms of expressing what you are truly capable of doing. This is being authentic, i.e. your capabilities in terms of identifying and solving problems, providing the right solutions, making appropriate decisions and being honestly accountable for your results; in short, being able to make an objective analysis, between what has been achieved and what is lacking, what has been achieved and the agreed-upon goal.

If with your attitude, you exaggerate your capacity of what you are truly capable of, and you do not achieve the expected results, you pay a price: you lose credibility.

CHAPTER I – CULTURE OF TRUSTABILITY

If with your attitude, you underestimate your own capabilities, and out of fear, you do not advance, because you underestimate yourself, you pay a price: you will not be able to aspire to have high credibility in that profession.

In short, be ethical and honest when talking about yourself, willing to check what you say about yourself. This is the first step of Trustability. Be honest with yourself and express to others what is truly true, and you can show it with the pleasure of doing so.

Let's clarify the difference between Trustability and Performance.

- Trustability is to be competent in what you say, ethical in your results and in your personal life.
- Performance is performing the job as is, without considering the inherent truths about your attitude and human side; that is, your integrity, your personal life, your ethics are not taken into account.

The thesis of this book is that sooner or later, personal Ethics also affects the tangible results of performance; that is, personal life affects Trustability and influences professional life.

A recent and worldwide example is Tiger Woods, world famous golfer, who for ethical reasons in matters outside his trade, lost some contracts with his sponsors, which later also affected his professional game, lowering his performance.

In other words, it is worthwhile, when agreeing on expected performance results, to include or not, aspects of Ethics and Honesty, together with aspects of technical performance in the trade. Some of Tiger Woods' sponsors did include it and some did not.

In this book we sustain the thesis that at least, aspects of Ethics and Honesty that have to do with the execution of the office should be considered in the performance; not to falsify anything in its accountability. It is recommended that those aspects of Ethics that are of personal life, that come to public light and that impact the company, should also be considered and merit sanction.

DIFFERENCE BETWEEN TRUST AND RESULTS

Trustability is having good, accurate results most of the time.

The results obtained may be poor, fair, or good.

This objectivity about the results obtained is basic to understand and adopt the culture of BEING A TRUSTWORTHY PERSON, that is, to be able to understand and apply the systems and criteria proposed in this book, to develop Trustability, especially when we undertake the implementation of the *Model to Build Trust*.

SPECIFIC OR MARGIN SITUATIONS

In real life, there are precise situations, where there is only one concrete, discrete answer: *YES* or *NO*, period.

- In precise situations: you are either pregnant or you are not, period; there is no in-between. Whether or not you are sick with any disease. Were you in x place at this time or not? You did or did not take the object at x time, on x day. When it happens that you arrive at x speed and with x aircraft, with x conditions of temperature, humidity and wind, the aircraft takes off or does not take off, at the correct pull of the control.

The ball is either in the playfield or out of the playfield, period.

- What exactly did you offer, did you deliver? This is the universal factor of Trustability in the World of Precise Situations.
- In the case of musicians, Trustability can be measured for note accuracy, precise *timing*, rhythm, sound intensity, harmony, and integration with other sounds.

YES or *NO*, period. If the answer is NO, the question now follows: How much of the 100% did you *DO* meet and how much did you *NOT* meet?

Your perception is important, and more important, is the perception of others involved and affected.

In precise situations, Trustability is measured by being accurate, which means, that what you say, sticks to the truth, sticks to objectivity, and can be checked. In these cases of Precise Situations, there are 3 options:

1. Assert forcefully, prove it, and get it right according to the truth.
2. Assert and be wrong in what you assert, according to the truth, for what you say is not the truth.
3. Say I don't know, or I'm not sure. If in doubt, it is better to use this option and then investigate.

In margin situations, wide, where there are several concrete, correct, and possible answers, of measurement or judgment in the World of the probabilities of occurrence, especially when it refers to future proposals. However, the statistical world is also useful when applying the concept of probabilities of occurrence of possible causes in the past and their estimated or defined proportion.

An example of Margin situations in baseball where there is a margin to hit well, as there is an opportunity for three balls and two *strikes*, before the outcome of the precise result. In sports, there is a field of *fair play* and an *offside* . Within the field of *fair play*, multiple moves or plays can be made, successful or unsuccessful. The Trustworthy person, whether or not they get it right, within that possible playfield, within that margin of action, for a significant outcome. On the *offside* field, any attempt, movement, or play is not valid, is not allowed and does not count (this is a precise situation). In addition, Trustability is measured by accurate results. It can also be expressed as the percentage of successful moves out of the total number of attempts made.

Another view, in margin situations, is how long you stayed within the *fair* field and how many significant achievements you made.

With the above examples, I wanted to give a technical analysis of Trustability, displaying *score achievements,* on the one hand, and *achievements that are significant and generally, producers of a better final result or higher score*, on the other hand; all seen integrally. Back to the point, being trustworthy is not easy. Especially in complex fields of activity.

I took sports as an example, but in a company, business and professional trades also have a playing field and results that are generally more complex than sports: Client and sales management, with its intermediate phases; material and supplier management, with its intermediate phases; employee workforce management and its intermediate phases; management of efficiency, profitability, and growth results; asset management and its evolution; and finally, management of social impacts.

What is Trustability like in general, in the following social fields?

- Federal, state, and municipal public administration.
- Army
- Police
- Politics
- Family
- Children's education, schools, and universities.
- Medicine and health.
- Athletes.
- Aviation.
- Road transportation.

In the culture of our society, do we deliberately encourage Trustability, or do we let it happen randomly, or do we deliberately discourage it?

If you stop to think, you can see that some areas of human activity are more sensitive than others. There are some fields where Untrustworthiness causes human deaths, for example in aviation and medicine. In other fields, Untrustworthiness produces indirect deaths or injuries. In the administrative field, mistakes often cause death-like effects, as they leave deep human damage.

In probabilistic situations, when it comes to giving an opinion, betting, or discussing the foreseeable future, no one is God to know what will happen with accuracy, truth, and objectivity. However, we see that it is very common for many people to say and assert what will happen on certain topics or issues.

In this regard, I dare to classify people as follows:

1. Those who confuse the *I want it to be*, with *what it really is*. These people assure what is going to happen, without notions of probability or objectivity.

2. Those who know that things can change in seconds and recognize that, until it happens, it is safe; they know how to differentiate between *what I would like to happen*, and *what really happens* or *can happen*. These people talk about what they expect to happen, because they can visualize it, understanding that they cannot guarantee it. Surely, they will do something proactive that may cause what they desire and envision, but they know it is not 100 percent certain. They are able to understand the probabilities of occurrence, they can undertake assurance, so that they increase in what they intend.

3. Those who live in the present and have not developed their visionary-strategic thinking process to penetrate probabilistic, possible future occurrences and their implications, prefer to say: *I have no idea, I don't know,* or I *don't care*.

As you can see, only people in group 2 have the raw material and potential to be Trustworthy in the World of Probabilistic Situations.

People in groups 1 and 3 need to develop their visionary-strategic thinking process, along with their objectivity (qualities of Emotional Intelligence), in order to move to group 2 and have Trustability.

Not many people are well trained to have this probabilistic thought process in their decision making.

6- WHO CAN YOU BE TRUSTED BY?

Do you have Credibility? In which subjects or trades?

Ask yourself if you are Trustworthy in certain subjects or trades, in the perception of others, in the perception of those around you, in the perception of those who have and master your trade.

The perception of others is not always one hundred percent correct. It depends on the prejudices and ability to master the profession of the person who is going to qualify and judge.

Generally, your opinion of your Trustability alone is very poor. Of course, there are exceptions, when the degree of *expertise* and demand is very high and, with that degree, you judge yourself; then, it turns out that your judgment is better than the judgment of others. However, the answer lies with those around you, and you exchange give and take; it lies with third party experts of your trade.

- Are you trustworthy?
- To whom?
- In what aspects or topics are you Trustworthy, and in what topics do you not seem Trustworthy, in the perception of others?
- Are you and have you been trustworthy with your family, have you not failed your children, your parents, your siblings?
- Are you trustworthy in general?
- Are you trustworthy in your occupation or main activity?
- Are you trustworthy in everything you offer or promise?

- With your superiors (parents, teachers, bosses).
- With your colleagues (siblings, friends, neighbors).
- With your colleagues at work.
- With your clients.
- With your partners.
- With your suppliers.
- With your partner.
- With your children.
- With your collaborators when you have people under your command.

Deep in your heart and in your conscience, you can answer these questions, evaluate yourself, applying a scale of *high*, *medium high*, *medium low*, *low,* and *null*.

But it's good to have their perspective. The ones who have the say about your Trustability are not you, but others, with whom you relate to in the giving and receiving of something. Ask and investigate, in which subjects do they trust you and in which ones they don't trust you.

It is the first step on the journey to *becoming more trustworthy* in whatever you set your mind to. And this information will give you the platform to educate your *self*. The idea is that, in the end, you are the best judge of your own Trustability. But for that, you need training in objectivity, and in the perceptions of others who see you perform and, if you ask, give you a great reference.

If you are Trustworthy to others and set that example, it is very likely that they will respond to you in the same way, being Trustworthy themselves.

Imagine how much a country could save on re-checks and paperwork established by Untrustability.

Then comes the question:

Is it poverty that prevents you from being efficient? Or rather, does lack of efficiency and productivity cause poverty? Untrustability produces inefficiency and poverty.

Imagine... if we have a country where everyone fulfills what they promise, the progress it would have, and the consequences in human relations, trust, optimism, objectivity, the satisfaction of living well, etc.

The Culture of Trustability consists of BEING TRUSTED BY OTHERS WITH WHOM YOU INTERACT: that is, that you are Trustworthy in the eyes of others.

7- WHEN IS TRUST LOST?

Confidence is gained slowly, like the growth of the palm, and lost quickly, as when the coconut falls from the palm.

We must understand that, in order to be Trustworthy, one must be Ethical and, in addition, Responsible and good (accurate) in the exercise of the trade or subject in question.

Trustability is lost or not gained when:

- Subjective, biased, and tendentious judgments are made to favor themselves.
- You have that inheritance and that habit of deceiving, knowing that the reality is different; you seek to

deceive to favor yourself or someone else. In other words: the truth, you use it when it suits you and favors you, and when it does not suit you, you use deceit.

- Out of ignorance, or because you thought it was so, when in fact it is not so.
- You confuse the problem, the symptom, and the wrong solution.
- When you don't get the right solution.
- When you underestimate the problem, you underestimate the other person to whom you are answering or providing a service.
- When you commit injustices.
- When you lack adequate information to decide.
- When you lack a capability that is relevant to the topic or issue at hand and do not make it apparent in advance.
- When you are ill or unable to act, you do not report and refrain from participating responsibly.

COVID is a relevant problem that affects everyone and is very illustrative when talking about Trustability. It is important to illustrate the following list with examples:

- New Zealand, Denmark, Japan and then Germany are good examples of Trustability.
- The United States, with a history of achievement for its dedication to providing the best solutions and progress, this time failed to be one of the most trusted on the planet. But they reacted and controlled better.

CHAPTER I – CULTURE OF TRUSTABILITY

- Mexico acted in an inferior manner and, in my opinion, lowering the level of Trustability, with respect to themselves, in the same manner as in the United States. Both countries had a history of greater Trustability in similar problems and issues.

- Spain and Italy, at least at the beginning of the pandemic, showed very poor Trustability due to their very poor results.

- Latin America has shown low trustability in general.

Low Trustability goes beyond having bad results. Low Trustability, it shows that their internal processes to achieve results are so bad, weak, or twisted, that it can be predicted in the future; that their results will continue to be bad, if they do not change their ways of planning, doing, and controlling things. Having said the above, I point out in the COVID topic, some possible causes, which have to do with what I have already mentioned, where I highlight, *What makes you lose Trustability or not gain it?*

- Neglect of the problem (putting off until tomorrow what should be done today).

- Incompetence in the problem and solutions.

- Withholding information from real and objective data.

- Inability to obtain relevant data and information.

- Confusion when attacking technical problems with ideological solutions.

- Ignorance of managers in the handling of statistics and data curves, confusing others.

- Absence of the culture of reacting in time, removing causes of inefficiency and errors.

- Placing unsuitable people in assigned responsibilities.

What can be observed in this list of causes that generate low Trustability, that prevent good results, is that they are causes, factors of diverse nature, technical, human and of social organization and then, it forces me to say that Trustability requires technique, character, discipline, and high values that we are far from having a solid Trustability. Therefore, the culture to build a solid and sustainable Trustability takes time to develop. However, the fruits of improvement and human satisfaction are harvested very quickly, that is, from the first steps of the methodology.

8- ANTIDOTES TO LOW HUMAN TRUST

Consciousness nourished by the spiritual that ancient cultures have brought to the world:

- Hindu Buddhism.
- Derivatives of Buddhism in China.
- Derivatives of Buddhism in Japan.
- Christianity.
- Derived from Christianity.
- Philosophy of English honorability.
- Natural kindness avoiding envy, from the Rarámuri culture.
- Natural goodness of some indigenous cultures.
- Laws based on honorability and conventional and agreed justice.
- Codes of Ethics.

- High levels of Consciousness.
- Sports rules and regulations to govern sporting contests.
- Internal work regulations.
- Laws or regulations controlling potential Conflicts of Interest.
- Ethical Audit (Conflicts of Interest).
- Universal human rights.
- Scientific verifications.
- Certified technical measurements.
- Surveillance with cameras everywhere.

9- WHAT IS REQUIRED TO ACHIEVE INSTITUTIONAL TRUST?

Capitalizing on mistakes and learning from them; taking references from more Trustworthy cultures, both from our own country and from other countries that are recognized for their Trustability; researching and deepening in what we do want to be in order to improve; and, having experienced models to develop Quality and Trustability, we can obtain a *Model to Build Trust*.

In Japan, the culture comes from 3 factors: a ruling class of an imperial family, which does not need to fight and win over others to stay in power; a Buddhist culture of humility and service; a decision of the ruling class, which consists of all the people as a whole, all Japanese citizens, have been developed in the service of others, thinking of a united and collaborative country. It is the only country in which the

Buddhist practice of humility was not only applied for personal development but is practiced as social development to think and collaborate in the wellbeing of others.

In the world of work, companies that have deepened in *Quality Models* have implemented a series of factors that are being learned, and then, developed, achieving greater trustability in their products and processes to do the job. Certain factors are required to be Trustworthy, which are shown in the *Quality Models*, and if people in the world of work apply these factors, then they will be able to set an example to others, in the normal and social life of everyone. That is, as a purchaser and beneficiary of certain work products, you receive a Trustability education. This Trustability education could be a good example to follow in education and development.

The idea of this book is to increase interest and competence to achieve greater Trustability. What I suggest is to educate based on the Trustability Models that we will discuss in the next chapter, so that each person first adopts them and then adapts them to their own circumstances.

CHAPTER II
MODEL TO BUILD TRUST HO

The increase of Trustability in societies, in human relations, has as its purpose an exchange of goods between each other. This exchange of goods can be between two or an unlimited number of persons. Generally, there are companies, institutions or organizations that are set up to facilitate these exchanges of goods.

I will now set out the 20 key factors required to facilitate and achieve Trustability, which includes people, organization, work systems which, in turn, groups functions, processes, information technology and Trustworthy management, with oversight and governance practices from the highest level.

I designed the *Model to Build Trust HO*, based on my experiences of 53 years of professional life, going through very different specialties: Mechanical Engineering; Master's Degree in Management; Specialization in Labor Psychology and Organizational Development; Design of Organizational Structures; Human Capital Management; Quality Models; Total Corporate and Manufacturing Quality; Market Intelligence; Strategic Planning; Emotional Intelligence; and Institutional Leadership.

The letters *HO* are written to reflect that this Model is *HUMAN ORIENTED* or *HUMAN AND ORGANIZATION ORIENTED*.

The idea is first to establish it *conceptually* and then to derive it into more concrete and specific models for each company, according to its line of business and circumstances, accompanying this *Model to Build Trust HO* with *coaching*, courses, and consultancy, to help society to have more competencies in these functions and specialties that increase Trustability.

The idea is to put it in a universal language, in such a way that it can be understood by leaders and collaborators, leaders and those being led, so that everyone can be motivated: older people, adults, young people and even children, with practical exercises that illustrate this *Model to Build Trust HO,* with its sections and its *20 factors* to be implemented, fostering an institutional and trustworthy culture.

SCHEMATIC SYNTHESIS OF THE MODEL TO BUILD TRUST HO

SCHEMATIC SYNTHESIS OF THE MODEL TO BUILD TRUST HO

II.1. MANAGEMENT COMMITMENT AND AWARENESS RAISING

1. LEADERSHIP COMMITMENT TO THE MODEL TO BUILD TRUST HO, FROM THE HIGHEST LEVEL
2. AWARENESS/PREPAREDNESS

II.2. IMPLEMENTATION OF THE MODEL TO BUILD TRUST

F1. COLLABORATION AND SERVICE TO OTHERS

F2. COMMITMENT/ORGANIZED WILL

F3. INSTITUTIONAL LEADERSHIP

- F3.1. Basic responsibilities
- F3.2. Management/Delegation Modes
- F3.3. Openness in Decision and Authority Perspectives
- F3.4. Moral Authority and Formal Authority

F4. VISION/STRATEGY

F5. CONCEPT OF CUSTOMER AND USER, AS WELL AS SUPPLIER. SUPPLIER-CUSTOMER-USER CHAIN

F6. CARE FOR THE CUSTOMER AND THE USER

F7. CONNECTION

F8. PLANNING BEFORE EXECUTING

F9. DEPLOY, STREAMLINE, AND CONTROL INPUTS

F10. EXECUTION AND TESTING

- F10.1. Four Worlds in Execution
- F10.2. Basic objectives to be achieved in World 1 of the Execution
- F10.3. Thinking, Feeling, Acting and Checking
- F10.4. *HO Method* to achieve Excellence Objectives
- F10.5. Fields of Emotional Intelligence
- F10.6. Exercise your Freedom by choosing your Vocation
- F10.7. Continuity vs. Disruption by innovation
- F10.8. Verification
- F10.9. Execution in World 3, the Staff World
- F10.10. Execution in World 4, the World of Judges

- **F11. QUALITY CONTROL**
  - F11.1. Quality Control Approaches
  - F11.2. Inspection
  - F11.3. Process Control
  - F11.4. Quality as a *Staff* Function
- **F12. EXCELLENCE IN BUSINESS CONTINUITY**
- **F13. FAULT DETECTION AND LEARNING FROM MISTAKES**
- **F14. MEASUREMENT AND DOCUMENTATION**
- **F15. CONTINUOUS IMPROVEMENT AND INNOVATION**
  - F15.1. Innovation Processes
  - F15.2. Continuous Improvement
  - F15.3. Process Modification
  - F15.4. Process Reengineering
  - F15.5. New Product Development
  - F15.6. Innovation Projects
  - F15.7. Research and Development
- **F16. CONTINUOUS COMMUNICATION OF RESULTS AND VALUES**
- **F17. PRACTICAL POLICIES, LAWS AND REGULATIONS**
- **F18. AUDIT**
- **F19. HUMAN DEVELOPMENT STRATEGIES**
  - F19.1. Trustability Achievement Recognition
  - F19.2. Participatory Socio-Technical Leadership
  - F19.3. The Right Person in the Right Position
  - F19.4. Continuous Training in the Trade
  - F19.5. Continuous Training on the *Model to Build Trust HO.*
  - F19.6. Emotional Intelligence Training
- **F20. HUMAN MOTIVATION STRATEGIES**
  - F20.1. Promotion of Values and their Application in Each Position
  - F20.2. Physical and Emotional Health Promotion and Care
  - F20.3. Development of Work Purposes
  - F20.4. Equity and Transcendence Environment

II.3. MANAGEMENT OF THE MODEL TO BUILD TRUST HO.

II.4. CONFLICTS OF INTEREST

II.5. COMPLEMENTARY EXPLANATIONS TO THE MODEL

1. WHY SHOULD WE BE TRUSTWORTHY?

2. **CONSEQUENCES OF BEING TRUSTWORTHY**
3. **CONSEQUENCES OF NOT BEING TRUSTWORTHY**
4. **LEVELS OF TRUST**
5. **CHAIN OF LINKS TO BE COVERED, IN ORDER TO BE A TRUSTWORTHY ORGANIZATION**
6. **ORGANIZATION TO INCREASE THE COMPANY'S TRUST**

II.1. MANAGEMENT COMMITMENT AND AWARENESS RAISING

1. LEADERSHIP COMMITMENT TO THE MODEL TO BUILD TRUST HO, FROM THE HIGHEST LEVEL

As we have been discussing in this book, leadership is the most important factor to achieve Trustability, we must ensure that, in the practice of leadership, the following is very clear: it is not valid to say: *you are trustworthy and loyal to me and take these rules and systems to be trustworthy and I lead and supervise you*.

This is not the way it is and should not be.

He and leaders at the highest level must understand and practice it. They must submit to Trustability Assurance systems in their leadership.

The leader and leaders at the highest level must be trusted by third-parties, both inside and outside their organization, starting with their clients, suppliers, and the community.

It has been proven that a large part of the population imitates their bosses or superiors, not because of what they say and preach in their speeches, but because of their actions and decisions. *Facts*: this is what makes up true communication. *Facts*: they are love and not just good intentions. The language of *Acts* is well understood by all people.

A *fact-based* narrative is the strongest part of the communication required from the leader to enter into establishing a Trustability Assurance Model in the company.

2. AWARENESS/PREPAREDNESS

1. As a first point: understand, buy the idea, and internalize the mystique of Trustability and take the vocation of Trustability.

2. Understanding the *Definitions of Being a Trustworthy Person*.

3. Understanding the *Ethical Causes of Trustability*.

4. Understanding the *Binomial of Fundamental Elements to be Trustworthy*.

5. Understanding the *Anthropological Basis of the Trustworthy Person*.

6. Have a defined scope of action to implement the Trustability Assurance Model, explaining some areas for improvement for which the Model is justified.

7. Motivate the effort and the journey through the *Model to Build Trust*, based on the expected benefits for the company and for all.

II.2. IMPLEMENTATION OF THE MODEL TO BUILD TRUST

F1. COLLABORATION AND SERVICE TO OTHERS

First, to do one's own activity well; then, to succeed in facilitating the activity of others; then, to be available to collaborate in extras. An excellent example is baseball, which applies to all jobs: picking up the ball by the second baseman, doing his role correctly, but also throwing the ball to third base, so that it is received comfortably and getting the *out*, facilitating the work of the third baseman.

Spontaneous collaboration, hospitality and friendship are signs of appreciation for others. When these signals exist in cultures, it makes it much easier to add trustworthy performance for the benefit of others. In these cultures, I change the word *Trustability* to "*Trustkindnessability*", and it is a very precious fruit of that society.

This mystique of work and service must be instituted, this mystique of Collaboration must be transmitted.

We need to develop more love for our profession or specialty, give that extra of collaboration and service, love for the company's T-shirt or place of work, and honorability in the healthy competition with the adversary, to reach the desired level in the *Model to Build Trust*.

When we come from a history of Low Trustability, citizens distrust the government and the government distrusts the citizens; collaborators distrust their bosses and bosses distrust their collaborators; colleagues distrust each other;

adversaries, with greater reason, distrust their opponents when there are competitions and, both, distrust the referees.

The handshake of ancient times, between two honorable and well-known persons, is an example of High Trustability and, also, a good example of efficiency in the process.

Today, in the 21st century, a more sophisticated system is required to ensure Trustability, being a larger group of people collaborating or working with each other.

Now, more sophistication in people management is required, with the following people management processes:

- Clarify individual roles.
- Share the scope of the project in the group of people.
- Clarify doubts in the group.
- Design, each one, what they recommend to change for themselves.
- Call for the undertaking of those proposed changes and agree on them in consensus, with efficiency and good coordination of the facilitator.
- Test, pilot and then implement.
- Give recognition for achievements, both individually and as a group.

This means transforming processes to be less bureaucratic and costly, but having more Trustability, more education in Trustability, in order to be more successful, more competitive.

More people and more trustworthy processes, with intelligence, results in less bureaucracy, less controls, because each step of the process and of the production chain is self-regulating and self-checking.

This should be done in the group of first and second level leaders, that is, among colleagues in the circle of leaders at the highest level, and thus avoid the tremendous divisions caused by the bosses at the bottom.

There are people who never learned to collaborate with others, who never belonged to a team as a whole, where strategy, actions, triumphs, and failures had to be shared. In these cases, it is necessary to lead them wisely, taking the help of those who do know how to collaborate as a team, showing examples and results. In addition to *coaching* them.

ASSISTANCE TECHNIQUES: Role Clarification; *Team Building* Sessions , oriented to the socio-technical work system; Human Profiling; Identification of informal leaders; Emotional Intelligence applied to work; Organizational Climate; Teamwork Development (Pilot and Co-pilot Work Aviation Case); Quality Training; Trustability Training; Awareness for the motivation to collaborate.

F2. COMMITMENT/ORGANIZED WILL

People are free and, if by their own free will, they do not accept to play, do not accept to work, do not accept certain rules to work, it does not represent a benefit, a satisfaction, a felt need, then, it must be said, and better to do what they are convinced, instead of being forced and resentful. By force, it backfires. In the culinary world, it is said that if the person has bad will, is emotionally disconnected, sad or angry, the dish cooked turns out badly and harms the person who eats it. In the field of aviation, also, pilots are advised not to fly when there is emotional instability, it is unsafe. In the sports environment of high competition and performance, it is the same, you are not going to be able to win when you are emotionally unwell.

Something similar happens with any work, where, if there is a bad emotional disposition, the deliverable of that work, as well as the dish that comes out of the kitchen, comes out bad, harmful, counterproductive, if the attitude of the producer or the receiver is negative.

Therefore, it is necessary to ask the participants: Do you want to do it, do you do it out of obligation, forcibly and against your will? First, it requires willingness, motivation, and vocation to participate and, in addition, the desire to learn more and do it better.

We need to awaken a taste for the obligations that correspond to each personal work situation, which are voluntarily accepted, and which generate internal satisfaction and motivation for the meaning that doing them represents.

And where does that leave remuneration, which is a fundamental motivation for convincing someone of a job?

It is important to note that there is no remuneration that solves a problem of internal demotivation. When demotivation is permanent, it makes you sick. Remuneration helps to convince you to do such a thing, but only temporarily, because if your work makes you sick, no matter how much money you are paid, it will not cure your affliction.

In terms of motivation, according to *Maslow's Pyramid*: not everyone is motivated by the same thing, it depends a lot on the scale on which you have been covering your needs.

When there is a certain level of satisfaction in your physiological, food, clothing, and housing needs, then the next possible levels of motivation follow:

- Personal realization.
- Forming a family.
- Forming a company.
- Leave a lasting contribution footprint.
- Doing things that result in important meaning for you.
- Doing things for the pleasure of doing them, because they are hobbies and work at the same time.

I am referring to the World of *DOING*.

Not necessarily, everyone participates equally in the World of *DOING*. There are people more motivated by *doing* and others more motivated by *BEING*, by thinking, reflecting, as well as others who are more motivated by observing, talking, commanding, without performing tangible actions and deeds in the World of *doing*.

Thinking to say well is one thing and *thinking to do well* is quite another. The neural groups used for thinking are very different. It is very common to confuse that, by saying good, you do good, and many times, it is not true. The language to conduct the *doing* is very different from the one that conducts the criticizing, speculating, and imagining, very distant from the *doing*.

There are well-thought speeches to criticize, but not necessarily, whoever criticizes, has the competences and the adequate thinking to solve, favorably, those criticisms that they themselves produce with words and, many times, they are far from being able to provide solutions with actions.

In the Strengths of Mind course, these differences are clearly learned.

It is important, when talking about roles to do, to collaborate and with commitments, to know these motivations of people and to substantiate them with their personal background.

It is important to lead people in roles appropriate to their human profile. It is important to point out the areas of opportunity between the actual profile of the person and the profile required by the job, role, or position in the organization.

The job profile defines how it is and how it should be in the World of *Doing*. It is very good to define the position and the role that each one plays according to the following:

- World 1. The World of *doing*, of *line*, in real life (moments of truth): to execute with deeds, with actions that are noticed, that require mind, hands, legs, body and attitude.

- World 2. The World of giving guidance and orders with authority.

- World 3. The World of providing support and support *staff,* by *doing, line*.

- World 4. The World of the impartial judge.

In baseball, World 1 of doing, which I call line, is pitching, catching, fielding, hitting, batting, and running the bases. It is defined as persons who are in an authorized and valid position to touch and maneuver with the ball in play and who are responsible for achieving a good maneuver, a good destination of the ball.

The coach thinks, talks and guides, but does not bat, field, catch, pitch, or run the bases in the course of the game; that is, the coach does not act or execute in the moments of truth, of real life.

World 2, give guidance and orders with authority. The World of Command. Decide who plays which position.

Continuing with the baseball example, the doctor who cures injuries, the administrator who sells and collects tickets, are examples of World 3: the World of Staff.

The referees and judges who mark the results of the plays belong to World 4.

In companies, generally, World 1 is what I call: *the line*; it is defined by those participants who are involved in handling the product, from its production to its delivery to the client, by selling and negotiating. People who, because of their role, have a direct impact with their thoughts and actions in the direct sale, in the elaboration of some part of the product or service, up to its delivery.

World 2 is made up of managers of different classes and levels, but it should be clarified what part of their role is to have direct line actions, either with the product or with the client, and what part of their role, and with whom, is only to review, supervise and give guidance, without intervening. In most cases, it is a mix that needs to be managed very well, identifying these very different roles.

When the one who belongs to World 2 also operates in World 1, without any order or separation of these roles, it usually causes many conflicts. There is a conflict when an error or failure results. Whose fault is it, who caused it, was it on purpose, carelessness, or lack of training?

The bosses' defensive attitudes are very strong: they do not want to lose their job and use their authority to ensure that it is not their fault.

There is a Conflict of Interest when you are judge and party, in deciding who did it and in deciding the corresponding sanction.

Under the *Model to Build Trust HO* approach there are 3 premises:

1. The boss must absorb *the blame*, or rather, *the responsibility* to properly handle those mistakes, to prevent them from being made again, when the failure was caused by someone in that area that the boss commands.
2. It must be investigated, objectively (motivation for the truth), if it is due to the failure of the team process, lack of training, lack of clear guidelines from the bosses, the person, or the group itself, who had or had an oversight either by distraction or fatigue, or an action of someone with malice.
3. We must prevent it from happening again by learning from mistakes or failures and solving the root cause.

The probability that the cause of the failures is not due to malice is extremely high. This means, then, that we should not look for culprits, but for causes, most of the time. Even in case of malice, it is recommended to go to the root cause and see why he did it, what prompted them to do it. Sometimes, the temptation to make a mistake is great, and it is convenient to eliminate this cause of temptation in order to solve the problem, taking into account human frailty.

The commitment to think, act and deliver the outcome, at moments of truth, of World 1; the commitment to think and decide to guide, without being judge and jury in World 2; the commitment to think and act at appropriate moments, to support, but not interfere inappropriately, of World 3; and the commitment to think and decide the outcome of actions, without intervening in the play, of World 4; are all very different in character.

When there is confusion in these commitments, which is very common, due to a lack of understanding of each one's role, it causes many deficiencies that negatively affect Trustability.

The deficiency, in the clarity of roles, causes Type 1 Failures, due to confusion; for example, when it is said: *I thought it was your turn*. When the boss decides it, he accustoms the others to the fact that this decision always falls to the boss; by accustoming them in this way, he causes an unproductive and unnecessary dependence. Or *is that you told me to do so,* is another example.

It also causes Type 2 Failures, due to ambiguous or political approaches: *I do my role wrong, so that I can always get out of the problem*; when there are successes, it says: *it was me*; when there are failures, *it was someone else*. This seriously affects the reliability of the company since the managers represent the company and its culture.

Both types of failures negatively affect Trustability due to lack of properly understood Commitment.

The commitment of the chiefs of World 2 is definitely broader and more complex in relation to those in World 1 (without any command) and those in World 3 and World 4.

The human profiles of each of these 4 roles are different and, many times, conflicts occur that negatively affect Trustability and also the healthy culture of the company, if they are confused and interfere with each other, without unity of command and disorder.

It is always very good to turn to the *Duty to Be*. First, to whom the role corresponds if that role is sufficiently clear. If not, then correct it and clarify it for the immediate future.

Sometimes, the result is not good because of conflicts between the participants of these 4 Worlds, who fight for medals and misrepresent their role. Imagine in an orchestra: the guitar, the violin or the drums trying to beat the piano. That's how absurd it is when someone snatches the role of their partner. This is a serious error that makes for a bad result. Even the best baseball player can't cover third and first base, it's impossible, because they will lose the game because they can't. Thus, in the company and in real life, wanting, because you are very good or have a lot of power, to fill two positions that are impossible to fill in the appropriate time, is automatically lowering Trustability.

It is good to know and be able to cover other posts or positions, especially when they are close and during moments of truth and continuity of the operation, so that, in case of emergency or difficult situations, it is possible to collaborate and reinforce, but always in an interim, emergency, and temporary capacity, without attacking the colleague, but collaborating.

For there to be Trustability, there needs to be a good overall result and good individual results in each role in the 4 Worlds.

The Right and Trustworthy thing to do is for everyone to love their role, have passion, commitment to their role and be competent; without interfering with, or conflicting with, the other roles, so that the overall result is Trustworthy.

The Commitment of those in World 1 is to always win now and, during the operation or the game.

The World 2 Commitment is to win now and design what is necessary to secure the future. It is the World responsible for the strategy and the future.

The World 3 Commitment is to take care of the environment of each specialty that surrounds the World 1 participants, so that they can perform better and provide a favorable environment for the team.

The Commitment of World 4 is to be wise, impartial, fair, just, and right with the truth.

Different types of commitments that require deepening in the conduct and implementation of the Model to Build Trust, making better decisions to increase Trustability.

ASSISTANCE TECHNIQUES: Planning and establishment of an Organizational-Professional structure; Required Job Descriptions and Profiles; Communication and Organizational Development; Focus on Results; Process Engineering; Human Profiling; Organizational Survey; Corporate Governance; Institutionalization and Professionalization of the Company.

F3. INSTITUTIONAL LEADERSHIP

World 2, the World of Leadership, of Management, of the Command unit, generally has 4 major responsibilities, challenges, and commitments, which are encompassed in the following phrases:

F3.1. Basic responsibilities

1- To obtain good results from the institution in the present, for which it was created.

2- To know where to take the institution in the future; that is, to ensure its survival today and tomorrow.

3- Choosing, motivating, and developing a team that delivers results today, as well as being able to build for the future

4- Have the necessary technology and asset infrastructure (finance) in place to ensure the success of the present and future.

Institutional leadership is required, with a correct vision and a motivating and inspiring Emotional Intelligence. Good consensus management. Depth in knowing and feeling what is being handled, as if it were your own body. Just as your body responds to your thoughts, but also, and very strongly, responds to your feelings and resentments, so is the institution, the organization you run. And in the institution, thoughts are complicated, and feelings are complicated, being several or many people involved with different interests.

Partners, workers, clients, suppliers, government inspectors, clients' families and workers' families are involved. In English they are called *Stakeholders*. The leader is responsible for observing and influencing, for maintaining a positive harmony between giving and receiving from each of these highly influential audiences. Explicit or implicit consensus is fundamental for the successful management of institutional leadership.

Making decisions, sometimes with superior intellectual depth; sometimes with superior sensitivity; sometimes with superior listening skills; often with superior firmness; often deciding, accompanied by consensus; even deciding in the solitude of his office, gambling with his own skin.

Just as the body notices congruence or the lack of it, and gets sick when lack is continuous, so society notices Trustability and its lack. This has its consequences; so it is with the institution. An unreliable institution tends to disappear. The leader must have the qualities to think and feel these connections between the institution he or she leads and society.

The leader must be able to manage motivation and enthusiasm by convincing each of these audiences and must give attention to all of them.

There are two types of Leadership blunders: those that happen due to incompetence or carelessness, but do not cause embarrassment; those that happen and are done on purpose and cause embarrassment when detected and discovered.

A Trustworthy leader knows precisely what these limits are and avoids making decisions that could later cause them serious embarrassment in front of the family and loved ones they respect.

There are decisions in which there is a Conflict of Interest, which obliges the leader to sacrifice personal image for reasons of benefit to the institution; this does not cause embarrassment, it causes humility. This is being institutional. This is the case when you would like to favor someone close to you, but the institution establishes rules that do not allow you to do so, then, it is when you have to sacrifice face with your close one, but it benefits the institution. Of course, there is also the perspective that even in front of the person close to you, when there is nobility and dignity, it exalts you and you do not sacrifice your face.

In order to master and attend to these 4 great Responsibilities of the leader, referring to each of the 4 Worlds, and to attend to these involved audiences that reflect different perspectives, certain strengths of the mind and certain attributes of Emotional and Social Intelligence are indispensable.

To be at least tripolar, or quadripolar cerebrally and to handle the 4 types of thought processes with superiority:

1. Sufficient analytical depth to not confuse symptoms with causes and to be able to get to the root cause if required.
2. Depth in the course to be followed; that is, visionary but objective.
3. Intuitive depth to know how to authentically motivate and develop others, with sincere empathy and intuition to perceive danger and serious risks.
4. Logic and mental order to manage the day's time well, action plans to communicate clearly to others and to understand accounting.

There is a small population of strongly tripolar or quadripolar managers in the world, so it is important to learn to work as a team and to complement each other in order to achieve solid institutional leadership.

Finding in a single person all the ideal attributes for a position of high responsibility and complexity would lead to only 3% of the population being suitable. However, when working as a team, with two or three well-selected people, all these ideal attributes can be integrated into the whole.

In addition, the leader is required to be self-sufficient in providing for their own personal needs and have the time and desire to provide for the needs of others. Have sufficient personal energy. This is what guarantees to give more to the institution, instead of wanting to serve the institution they lead.

To be self-sufficient and deploy your energy towards satisfying the needs of others requires, from the point of view of Emotional Intelligence, the following:

- Objectivity.
- Independence.
- Pressure tolerance (postponing gratification).
- Impulse control.
- Emotional stability despite adversity.
- Feeling good about people and having others feel good about them.
- Inspire others.
- High internal need for self-fulfillment.

F3.2. Management/Delegation Modes

There are 4 ways to Lead/Delegate that, situationally, the Leader must choose at a given moment, and then know how to change at another moment, according to the life cycle (maturity) of the organization they lead, the leader's own life cycle and the life cycle of the people who occupy key positions in the organization.

1. Personally execute a part of the work of Worlds 1, 3, or 4, to teach and then, delegate those tasks to someone else to execute them, so as not to neglect the 4 major responsibilities of the leader already mentioned.

2. Establish the objective, the goal and the main action plans and lead them through the Direct Responsible, to whom they delegate the execution under orders and instructions.

3. To give general guidelines and request that the Responsible Parties formulate their objectives and action plans. Then, Listen, Advise, Conduct and Approve, or not approve the objectives and action plans. Then, monitor compliance. Evaluate success and trustability.

4. Provide guidance and coaching to ensure compliance with agreed objectives or make confident decisions on who to delegate to.

These 4 modes of leadership should be given depending on the life cycle and maturity of the people. The first mode, where people are novices in their positions; the second, when they are already at a low intermediate level; the third mode, when they are already at an advanced level; the fourth mode, when people have already become good at fulfilling their objectives.

F3.3. Openness in Decision and Authority Perspectives

Traditionally, orders flow from the boss to the next person in the hierarchical chain, in the form of instructions and orders, and that is the only channel of communication about *what I should* and *should not do*.

Under the *Model to Build Trust HO*, communication and delegation channels are expanded.

A good manager should have 5 Channels at their disposal to improve their decisions:

1. The traditional channel, where the boss says how, because they know and have experience.
2. The internal client Channel, next in the chain, when it is well connected in the production chain until it reaches the final external client. To know your needs, your specifications, your satisfaction.
3. The communication Channel, in the reverse direction of point 1. Ask before ordering: How would you do it, according to your experience and the training you have had?
4. The Expert *Staff* Channel, which advises from a technical point of view.
5. The Alternatives Analysis and Decision-Making Channel, which the job holder could develop when trained in the *Model to Build Trust HO*.

A good High Trustability manager knows and demonstrates, in practice, that they remain ultimately responsible, even when using the 4 additional channels. These 4 additional channels are a guarantee of success. If they feel involved and invited, it is much easier for the execution to go well. If they feel ownership of the decision for their participation, they will work to make it work. This is the best way to build consensus, to build solid consensus. Be trustworthy to others. The result is that the others will be trustworthy as well.

F3.4. Moral Authority and Formal Authority

It is very important, in Institutional Leadership, to avoid Conflict of Interest in everything and, especially, in the appointment of collaborators. Being institutional means deciding according to the profile demanded by the institution, not the convenience or personal taste of the leader. Likewise, decisions on the application of company rules should be institutional, not dependent on personal favors done for the boss in order to climb up the ladder.

The leader must be clear in their mind that the people they choose will have to answer for themselves and justify their position in front of everyone's eyes. If they cannot justify their appointment with the expected contribution results of the position, there will be a serious damage to the institution, both in terms of company results as well as a crisis in the work environment. In this case, Moral Authority goes to the ground along with its Trustability.

The boss who manages to have a Moral Authority by themselves, there is no doubt that the Formal Authority will perform it very well. They earn the right to be a leader, in addition to being a boss. However, the traditional formal boss may lack Moral Authority. Managers who only have Formal Authority, without having Moral Authority, are performing poorly in their position, and must be replaced by leaders with Moral Authority and Trustability.

This type of boss who has the Formal Authority, but does not have the Moral Authority, is a clear sign of institutional error and people notice it.

It is highly recommended, first, to observe and authenticate the Moral Authority, before giving them a position of boss, manager, or director. First, be their leader in some project and then, I will appoint you as their boss.

Moral authority is how consensus is achieved and, therefore, it should be how appointments are made. Moral Authority is earned when you are Trusted by them. In the case of the public, partners, customers, suppliers and inspectors, there is no relationship of subordination, so it is the Moral Authority that comes into play.

The Formal Authority confers authority to commit resources of the company, of the institution, and those decisions of high confidence must be granted to trustworthy people who have Moral Authority.

In the case of workers, staff, and collaborators, it is with the only public where managers can exercise continuous Formal Authority; but again, it does not serve to generate consensus and commitments of substance.

The Moral Authority is the one that allows to reach the soul, the heart, and the reason. It suits everyone; it is the seed that naturally sprouts and builds consensus.

ASSISTANCE TECHNIQUES: Leadership Styles; *Human Side and hsei* (Emotional Intelligence) Leadership Profiles; *PMI (People Management Institute)* Leadership courses ; Well-designed organizational structures.

F4. VISION/STRATEGY

The question must be answered: What is the *Mission* and *Vision* of the company from the highest governance body?

The company evolves with or without management. It is required, at this point, to have the *Vision* from the Management. In other words, the planning to be able to direct this evolution, so that it is as deliberate as possible. Considering that life evolves, and times change, what do you want your company to look like in 10 years in 4 Factors?

1. What is the goal? In which sea, in which league, in which cities, countries? What size?

2. With what *know how*? With what strengths and comparative advantages?

3. What do you want to be Trustworthy for?

4. With whom?

These 4 factors must be complementary and synergistic to be effective.

In addition, this 4-point vision must be communicated, discussed, and shared throughout the organization. Landing in each function, in each position.

The primary role of the leader is Vision and then, more importantly, it is with whom. Who are the best people (partners and collaborators) to make this Vision happen?

- How is the current level of Trustability?
- What happens, by doing what is being done, with low Trustability?
- Perhaps high inefficiency, high unnecessary cost, high demotivation of people in the organization, high customer dissatisfaction?
- What happens when you do it with a high level of Trustability?
- Lower supervision costs, higher productivity, lower production costs, higher client, and user satisfaction?
- Is there communication and consensus with the people regarding your Vision?

If there are no clear opportunities for improvement detected and the conviction of the benefits of the *Model to Build Trust*, there will be no energy to carry out the implementation of this MODEL.

- More satisfied and convinced clients of the company and its products.
- Employees who are more integrated and motivated to work in the company.
- Suppliers working in a more integrated way, with lower costs and greater satisfaction.
- Products and services that will raise your level of Trustability above that of your competitors.

The Vision, furthermore, is to contribute to generate a culture of Trustability at the country level. I mean, the education of the people is what allows us to have a better country, when this education increases Trustability. The education that is transmitted through work and business is, perhaps, more significant than that produced in traditional educational systems. This proposed Vision is to correct the negative trends of Trustability and reap its fruits at the country level, and then, at the company level, lower costs, reduce procedures, increase satisfaction and competitiveness nationally and internationally.

It requires Vision, that what you do is Trustworthy to build a better future, having clear the port you want to reach and the path to follow, thinking about the people to whom you will have to communicate, to give them understandable instructions for the next steps to follow, and not necessarily communicate the end of the path, especially when it is still far away.

It requires the Vision to work, act and operate within limits drawn by a more objective intelligence. This objective intelligence is potentially developed with the *Model to Build Trust*, its measurements, and pragmatic solutions for the benefit of others.

In *Section 8, Chapter I,* we talked about *Antidotes Against Low Human Trustability,* and many of these antidotes are of a spiritual nature.

I want to emphasize that happiness and fulfillment are a deliberate and conscious pursuit that is being insistently pursued in the 21st century. It is with thoughts of competence and social vision that we will achieve it.

In a tangible and evident way, the company cannot offer or achieve happiness and fulfillment, but it is a joint search: company and collaborator. Of course, the family and social life of each person is an important part of finding happiness and fulfillment, but work life is also very important. Combining both approaches, with Trustability and honesty, is the Strategic proposal of the *Model to Build Trust.*

The vision of the company that I propose is:

The company, offers to provide service with superior values to society, represented by its customers, collaborators, suppliers, and related community, being Highly Reliable and, as a consequence, all are benefited, extending this benefit to the whole country.

Values are a very valuable part of the Vision. This means that the Model must be very focused on the so-called *Ethical Causes of Trustability, Motivation for Truth* and *Perspective of the other* as an extension of itself.

These values strengthen and shield the person and the company from many bad practices and political manipulations, generating an education that employees use to increase productivity, service, and personal satisfaction, which they then transmit to their homes and families.

To make this a reality, it is necessary to deploy these values in the company, taking them to every department, to every position, to every corner of the company with repeatedly tested and useful methodologies.

There is a two-way correspondence: *the Tangible, which can be seen, and the Intangible, which can be felt*, must be in the *VISION*; the tangible, desired and feasible direction, with tangible well-being indicator measurements, are indispensable, but more important is the achievement of peace, happiness, and relevant human satisfaction, with emotional stability and enthusiasm; I am referring to the most essential human aspirations, aspiring to the highest levels of human well-being.

We need the leadership of each sector or area, and the visions they implement, to be able to combine this two-way correspondence of the tangible (which can be seen) with the intangible (which can be felt). We have yet to learn to manage the forcefulness of the tangible measured with the intangible well felt. That is to say, to bring about tangible, measured, honest and sustainable achievements, on the one hand, and on the other, with humane, prudent, and objective recognition. This should be one of the added values of the *Model to Build Trust*.

In terms of Human Capital and Human Profiles, we talk about balancing Assertiveness with Empathy; Push with Influence, Rational Intelligence with Emotional Intelligence. In our profile measurement statistics, we observe that there is a great imbalance that causes a great number of conflicts, lack of productivity and reliability.

We have a general situation quite common, where many leaders are either strong and good with the tangible, causing problems and disasters with the intangible and, finally, many unnecessary conflicts emerge; or they are good only with the intangible and cause many failures in achieving tangible achievements (what the client or shareholder sees).

The *Model to Build Trust* offers the added value of producing that balance so necessary for emotional balance, on the one hand, and on the other, the drive to achieve better products and services with better efficiency. Train and *coach* leaders to manage, in a natural way, the balance and two-way correspondence between the tangible and the intangible.

This is what is often mentioned in the 21st Century, we are going to see a fusion of the Eastern culture, sensitive and appreciative of the intangible, and the Western culture, which is careful to appreciate the tangible.

In Japan, from the time they are children, they are taught to live the 4 epochs of their life. This gives them balance, coming from nature itself, without the conflict of blaming others for what happens to them. Spring, Summer, Fall and, of course, Winter will come, and you have to prepare for the other 3 seasons. That gives vision and balance. It gives you direct responsibility for managing your destiny despite natural changes. It gives rational, objective intelligence, because it is seen; but also, it gives Emotional Intelligence because it is felt in the flesh, it is felt in parents and grandparents who are very dear to their children or grandchildren.

Projects, Consensus and Management.

Another issue to be clear about, from the Vision, is how to manage changes, disruptions, innovations, and projects, in balance with the continuity of the operation. Project, Consensus and Management. Project conceptualization and scope, strategic and financial feasibility, cost-benefit valuation as it relates to the project. Calling, convincing and involvement, with adequate information to the key people to be involved and engaged, as far as Consensus is concerned. And management processes to execute, control, deliver and account for their results and profitability. Project Consensus and Management are indispensable elements of administration to achieve Trustability in the leadership that directs the company.

In Japan, they have a lot of respect for change and for not affecting the continuity of the operation. So, with Projects, Consensus and Management, they achieve things efficiently and effectively. They manage to solve conflicting interfaces with education and proper planning. They manage very well the times of change with the times of consolidation.

In the *Model to Build Trust HO*, it proposes improvement and change to be more Trustworthy, more capable of being so, and lays the foundations of a path where it is possible, where everyone can, if they want to.

ASSISTANCE TECHNIQUES: Strategic Planning; SWOT; Mission, Vision and Values; Sector Study; Competitor Study; Market Research; Project Management; Management Structure; *Model to Build Trust*; Management by Objectives; Algorithms to create the Business Model.

F5. CONCEPT OF CUSTOMER AND USER, AS WELL AS SUPPLIER. SUPPLIER-CUSTOMER-USER CHAIN

It is necessary to identify your Client, that is, the person who has the power to request your intervention in something, whether it is a job, a project, a task, an assignment, a position.

The User is the person who makes use of what you deliver to your Client.

For example, if you sell a screwdriver to a factory, your Client is the one who decides to buy and pay you, but the User is the one who uses the tool you delivered.

This figure of Provider-Client-User is a very strong structure, so that if you remove or belittle any of the 3, the Trustability and then the interrelationship collapses. If you do not perceive the user's satisfaction with the screwdriver, and if satisfaction is low, they will complain and ask to buy another screwdriver. If you do not perceive the importance of the buyer, the relationship also collapses. Product-Client-User is another way to look at the structure, to understand and manage the right design, your right operation and your total Trustability.

To design a product or service, you better take the user into account and put yourself in their shoes.

In some places, I see a lot of confusion and difficulty in this, to distinguish a client from a user, and in the need to work more on user satisfaction and less on the Friend-Client-Provider collusion.

Many times, I see a lack of structure of the *Provider-Client-User* figure, and I see a *Provider-Friend-GIVE ME THE BUSINESS* figure.

And I ask: Who is the friend of whom? Should the client give the business to the provider because the provider is their friend? Or should the provider give them at cost the product/service or less, because the customer is their friend? Who is to be sacrificed for whom? 50/50?

Be careful, because this distorts *Trustability* and in the long run, tangible results leave their mark and history is in charge of repairing the errors of lack of Trustability.

This figure, *Provider-Friend*-GIVE ME THE BUSINESS, lends itself to be of Low Trustability, because those who work in providing the service and, above all, in receiving and approving the product or service from the client, are bound by personal commitments, far from the real business that should behave like this: *if you are good and better than your competition, in cost, quality, volume and service, I buy you*, otherwise, by discriminating against those who are good or better than you, you avoid development and quality. This is also corruption. They do not feel the pressure to do the job well, because it does not depend on their results, but on a friendship that they cannot control.

And among these Friends: How are they going to see who is the friend of whom? Who favored whom, at the expense of the other? How will the friendship remain if one of them *has assaulted* the other?

Sometimes, I observe in some cases, that the figure of *Provider-Client-User* is lost and there is only the figure of *Provider-Friend*.

The provider wants to become a client too, and decide about your product or service, as a client too, after all he is your friend. This shows signs of dishonesty and manipulated rules of the game. It is a base that shows signs of Low Trustability.

It also sometimes happens with the figure *Client-Friend*, instead of *Client-Provider*, where the client decides prices and costs, after all, the provider is his friend. Imagine the third parties involved, how they are left? Out of the game, but moving the ball, without being able to justify their correct performance, and trustworthy rules of behavior are lost and replaced by subjective political rules. This negatively affects Trustability.

Balance of delivering (Provider) and collecting (Client): balance of giving and receiving.

It is like the correct Breathing: *Inhalation = to put in external air = and exhalation = to take out internal air =.* Both are essential and one cannot be given without the other. If you do not inhale, you cannot exhale, and if you do not exhale, you cannot inhale steadily, but only momentarily.

When you have, you can give what you have; when you don't have, there is no way, you can't give. If you pretend to give what you don't have, you destroy yourself, and that is contrary to your well-being.

The idea of this game is to turn it into a virtuous circle: to *have more, in order to be able to give more,* and it is precisely where Trustability is a means of general enrichment. You and your neighbor benefit. Provider and Client benefit.

There is a central, fine, subtle point, where you, by giving more, receive more. This point is the second essence of Trustability, it is the derivative of offering the best. You offer the best, first essence, and receive more, second derived essence.

The more you deliver what you deliver and what you agreed to deliver, the more you receive now and the more you will receive later. This is the second essence of Trustability.

The first essence is the interaction between *Client-Provider*, in a process of giving and receiving, and the second essence is to turn it into a virtuous circle, where you receive more, have more and can give more, in a spiral of generating wealth and well-being.

The steps to carry out this *give and take*, in the Provider-Client-User figure, are at least the following:

1. Listening and knowing the client's request and needs from the provider. And on the client's side, be very clear on what they request and need, as well as their scope and resources to pay.

2. Specify the specifications of the deliverable to the client and the consideration for the provider. Agree with the client. It is the reasoned and free agreement between the parties that induces good results. It is not unilateral; it is bilateral or multilateral.

3. Work according to those specifications with measurement, accuracy, verification, and meeting client expectations, with positive and authentic emotions of appreciation and desire to serve.

4. Deliver as specified in time, manner, and cost. This requires work to prepare, produce and manage the product or service at issue. If you exceed your client's expectations, they become your promoter. That's leveraging your strengths.

5. Provide warranty support.

6. Receive the final payment from the client with positive and authentic emotions of mutual appreciation. If not, document what happened, analyze why there was insufficient satisfaction and correct, either for a post-sale deal with the current client or for future clients. There is always room for improvement.

In the end, it is a spiral of collecting more and delivering more for everyone's sake. Meet consumer demand with a good supply, and then enrich the supply and influence it to increase demand.

Happy, satisfied, and grateful clients for what they received, learned, and paid for; happy, satisfied, and grateful suppliers for what they delivered, worked, and received.

That in the end, the positive flavor of the interrelationship remains, beyond the economic issue. And if it is during the process of making the delivery or deliveries, so much the better.

CUSTOMER-SUPPLIER TRUST CONDITIONS		
CLIENT	SUPPLIER	POSSIBLE RESULTS
Honest and Competent	Honest and Competent	Give and receive with excellence, reciprocal correspondence, and gratitude.
Dishonest and Competent	Honest and Competent	Giving with excellence and receiving well, but wanting to *take advantage of*
Honest and Incompetent	Honest and Competent	GIVE with excellence and RECEIVE with gratitude, well, thanks to the Provider.
Honest and Competent	Dishonest and Competent	GIVE with subtleties and RECEIVE with full awareness of the client who measured the Provider.

Honest and Competent	Honest and Incompetent	GIVE with subtleties and RECEIVE with full awareness and subsidizing the provider.
Dishonest and Incompetent	Dishonest and Incompetent	GIVE with trickery and flaws *(gandalla)* and RECEIVE without paying *(gandalla)*.

Failures and mistakes can be corrected thanks to the honesty part of the equation and thanks to the competence part of the equation; it optimizes and enhances human relationships. When honesty and competence are not involved, human relations become impoverished and deteriorate, and society also becomes deteriorated.

There is an ocean of possibilities to innovate within these 6 steps already mentioned. They can always be done better and clearer, better, and faster, better and with less cost, better and with more guarantee, where provider and client benefit. It is in this space, where it is necessary to know how to act, developing more competences.

There is another space OUTSIDE THE ECUATION, further to the left, on one side, where the provider's abuse is found; and there is a space OUTSIDE THE ECUATION, further to the right, where the client's abuse is found. Those spaces I now called: OUTSIDE THE ECUATION is, as in sports, the lines OUTSIDE THE PLAYING FIELD, where a FOUL OR VIOLATION is committed. These OUTSIDES refer to possibilities of committing both honesty and competence faults. These fouls should be treated as in sports, with a yellow card first, and then a red card for repeated offenses or for serious offenses. This is a suitable system to increase

Trustability. The Measurement systems seen in *Factors 8, 9 and 10* should take care of this, initially, and then in *Factor 18: Audit,* as a convenient redundancy.

Many times, I hear the question, when I comment on all this complexity and all this effort: Why do I have to sacrifice so much for the client?

The answer is: put yourself at the end of the chain and you will be more than compensated, much more than you think at first glance. If your family buys products or services, in which you gave your effort and there were positive results of *Quality, Trustability and Satisfaction*, you will see that it is worth the effort to serve, because sooner or later, it will be returned to you. It is a collateral effect of social benefit that is then positively reverted to you, rewarding your positive influence on others, whether clients, users, or witnesses, which there always are. In addition, in this *Model to Build Trust,* there are *Factors 19 and 20*, where you will be able to observe and have a high degree of human, social, positive, and enriching treatment.

As a client, the following must be said, although it is certainly easier to receive than to give, to ask than to provide: the trustworthy client is the one who is not satisfied with just any product or service, but the one who knows their needs so well that they are able to choose their supplier very well, not only in terms of cost, but also in terms of opportunity costs. What is the point of being cheap if the performance and response time are not adequate?

In order to be a trustworthy client, it is necessary to know your own needs very well and to know, in a strategic way, the solution of problems and uses of your products and services that you need to be more Trustworthy in the future. With this deepening of the client, then, you have more productive material to drive the provider's efforts.

The provider needs a strategic and technical guidance to link its efforts with its client, to apply its product or service successfully, and it is where the client can better measure its potential suppliers in terms of being compliant, productive, and trustworthy.

Sometimes the client teaches the provider a lot; sometimes the provider teaches the client a lot. The important thing is that there is added value for both. When one of the two is totally passive, it is generally a sign of a probable lack of optimization.

This Provider-Client-User chain must be developed internally in the companies along the production chain itself, reestablishing internal interrelationships. It is not just the traditional chain of boss-subordinate, or as they say now, boss-collaborator. This unilateral chain is already insufficient.

Now, the process of how the product is elaborated until it is delivered to the final client must be formed, through the different steps in which the baton is handed over to someone else later on, depending on what each one adds value to. The internal client is the one who receives the message from the previous step in the chain. This internal client, of course, should check what they receive, and not start doing their job if there is something wrong in the previous step. Not waiting for the boss of the two to do that job, that is completely insufficient and inefficient.

The same can be done with services and processes that are chained together for a subsequent end result. In the construction industry, the product is the building, for example, and each one, each specialty, adds a part of the building.

Here, it is extremely useful to elaborate the internal chain Provider-Client-Internal because they are passing the baton, and of course it is convenient to institute the process of reception, delivery, and approval, by the internal client, regarding the previous work.

The Provider-Client-Internal chain, until reaching the End Client and User, is the most intelligent and efficient way to provide Trustability, quality, participative pride, and motivation at work.

In government agencies, with users and in public services, it is urgent to introduce this way of managing the Provider-Client-User chain, so that it becomes the mandatory culture, rather than, as is often the case now, being both judge and party, using the power of sanctions given to them by law to impose their ideas, ways of operating and treatment of people.

To all the above, we must add, in this 21st Century, networks and Internet, to avoid more inconveniences to clients and users, increase Trustability and customization, making the client participate a lot in the management of their own information, so that, in turn, they have a better service.

ASSISTANCE TECHNIQUES: The 6 Steps to organize the Provider-Client-User interrelationship are: Market Research; Market Intelligence; Satisfied Client Path; Client Evaluation; Client NPS; Voice of the Client; CR monitoring clients.

F6. CARE FOR THE CUSTOMER AND THE USER

It is required, at the level of belief, to love your client and your user, as the very thing that gives meaning to your work, to your effort, to your task. Your client, to a large extent, is the one who gives meaning and sense to what you do. Imagine what would happen if your relationship with your client started with you hating them: either you underestimate them or you despise them. It is very difficult, it would be going *against nature*, to give them a good service, a good product or a good deliverable. If you don't deliver something very good or you deliver something bad, the interrelationship can turn into a destructive and negative relationship, it would also be a boomerang that can turn against you.

It is necessary to measure the level of client satisfaction and undertake its improvement.

User satisfaction must be measured, and improvement must be undertaken.

The best way to acquire the practice of taking the client and the user into account is, first, to do the exercise with yourself.

If you were the client and you were the user, how would you like to be treated to be a promoter of your product, your service, your brand?

When the client of what you do is yourself, a rather interesting algorithm applies to you. You learn that giving and receiving are transformed.

You learn that giving is also receiving, since what you do to yourself and give to yourself, you are also receiving.

Then, working to give takes on a new meaning, and you enter a lane where you feel, in your own flesh, that giving is receiving; perhaps you receive more than what your client is receiving. You receive raison d'être of your work, sense of contributing to the well-being of others, learning a trade, new experiences, ways to solve problems. You consolidate a path of creating wealth for yourself (the more you have, the more you can give, and it multiplies), satisfaction for giving work to others, teaching others something that is useful and sustainable, a sense of accomplishment, reflections on how vulnerable life is and how you can lose if you don't work hard, moving with subtlety, caution, and prudence to avoid falling.

You learn that to receive is also to give, because today it is for you and tomorrow, perhaps, it is your turn to return some of what you received from someone else.

To put yourself as a resource (provider), and then, to change your cap for being the receiver or client, serves to understand that nature itself teaches you about life: spring and summer, to give many fruits; autumn and winter to endure, preserve and prepare for the next season; both extremes occur in the same year, it is the same nature that changes its role to give and deliver fruits, and then, to take care of what is harvested to consume it with good management.

It is good to separate *You as a Resource* and *You as a Beneficiary* of your own resources. Be good at both *You*: *You as a delivering resource* and *You as a receiving client*, aware of what it means to produce and give.

It is often more satisfying and enriching to be good, to consider yourself good, and to be considered good by others as a Resource, than to be good as a Beneficiary. For those who are good as a Resource, sometimes it gets boring to be good as a Beneficiary. They prefer to devote more time to their role of being a Resource to serve others, because it produces more satisfaction.

In other words, the ability to produce and deliver gives more satisfaction than the attitude of receiving.

On the contrary, he distrusts those who only see themselves as Beneficiaries of everything and shun their role of being good as a Resource, in order to serve others.

Giving and Receiving. Who will you trust the most with your life? To the one who wants and can give and a lot or to the one who only wants and can receive, and a lot?

Only children, the elderly, and people with circumstances of some disabilities, can afford to only receive and give little. Some, because they have already given, and others, because they are going to give.

There is a lot of potential to serve others and love others, but also, it must be said that, in the last twenty years, it has been nurtured in the culture of *Millennials*, where parents raised their children to always be served (receive and command), not so much to serve and obey. If what I have just said is too much emphasized, there is a risk that they may end up not being able to serve (inability to give) and this causes a very serious inner emptiness.

This *Millennial* culture education was made in all social strata with the help of television, which promoted this generation and the relaxation of family, academic and school disciplines. This directly motivates, that many of the *Millennials* only know how to be clients of others and not so much being hardworking and diligent suppliers.

However, there is already a *Generation Z*, which comes with a lot of entrepreneurial momentum, intelligence, good intentions to help and discipline. They already know, they have already realized from the results they observe in the lives of some *Millennials*, that it does not pay to just be served and go from party to party, to have all rights and no obligations.

He who does not live to serve, does not serve to live; be a Reliable Provider, of love, of useful products and services to your neighbor, children, parents, partner, neighbors, friends, formal or informal clients and you will reap blessings.

Provide something useful around you. Make informal clients, in addition to having your formal clients.

When you address your client, you as a provider, presuppose an attitude of service and of generating satisfaction in your client, that is the fundamental value of the Client-Provider exercise, it is the fundamental value of life. It is the engine of the Trustability culture. And it is contagious.

Apply this client concept to the people closest to you:

<u>To your parents</u>: see to some of their satisfiers and ensure their satisfaction, for they ensured your well-being when you were not self-sufficient. You were their client, and you got a lot. Nothing is free. It is your turn, in time, to be their provider. Be a grateful client for everything and start being a provider of some things and services for your home and family. Be a provider of cleanliness and tidiness of your room, of the house, so that later you can be a good provider when your parents can no longer provide for themselves. For sure, you will be able to induce this process with your children in the future.

<u>To your boss(es) at work</u>: you are an official and legal provider because of the agreements you have made with them. If you get paid for time, be diligent with that time, producing agreed-upon benefits. If you are paid for the product or service you deliver, try to exceed expectations. Be Trustworthy in terms of stating your progress in your process (Beginner, Intermediate, Advanced, Expert or Master), in a verifiable or certified manner. Don't base your work on how much you get paid; give the best you can, because it also develops you more. Be proud to have a job, to be a reliable supplier and seek continuous improvement of your services,

not only for the good of your company, your bosses, and your customers, but because you create an asset for yourself, with your good reputation, a personal brand in your services. Be Trustworthy, carrying out the entire *Model to Build Trust HO.*

Whatever you give extra, it will be capitalized sooner or later.

To your teachers: take care of giving them an answer in your assignments that makes them feel proud of their classes, so that they can see that you are improving and becoming a better person; this makes not only them, but also yourself, feel satisfied. Do something else in your answers that can be useful to your class and the next student generations, and if they have helped you in your improvement, let your teacher wear a medal for the good work done. Should the teacher fail to meet your expectations due to their irresponsibility, let them know at the appropriate time through the appropriate channel. Be a grateful client for the improvement you have made because of them. Be a demanding client, not satisfied with the irresponsibility.

To your partner: make sure you properly fulfill the role you have agreed upon; when there is a need to step out of that role, reach a consensus before making any changes. Almost anything is possible, if there is honesty of intention, good communication and negotiation. Your body expresses it in a more evident way than your words. Never betray their Trust. Always be trustworthy. By betraying their trust, you betray yourself. In this relationship, there is a very dynamic *switch* between being your partner's provider and being your partner's client. Give as a good, trustworthy provider and receive as a good, trustworthy, and grateful client. Therefore, the agreed role is vital. What are you in charge of, what is your partner in charge of, in terms of being providers? When in doubt, the best relationship I have found is that you both strive to be providers for each other, for the house and the family, because that is what works best, and in addition, you both strive for the other to be the client. More providing and less receiving, where there is doubt, is what works best.

It also doesn't work to fight about the other being the provider and you being the client unless it has been very well established in that agreed role.

<u>To your children</u>: you are the natural provider, measure what you give them of resources to live, so that they understand that, in this life, there are no free satisfactions. Even love needs to be nourished with reciprocal love; and it grows, otherwise it may wither. Love begins with getting to know the other person and realizing that they are different from you, and that what is different from you is sometimes good, not always bad, and that takes a lot of effort. Give them quality in your treatment when you are present. Teach them to be trustworthy suppliers, and as clients, to be grateful. Don't show them acceptance for the level of comfort and convenience. Don't teach them not to be providers, don't teach them to be overbearing clients. If you make the mistake of teaching them not to be providers, and to be high-handed customers, you are going to be the one who gets hurt, and not only you, but those around your children in their lives. Become a demanding client in the tasks you give them; be demanding but give them *coaching*. That they learn to always fight, to make mistakes, to correct and to get it right. Teach them the *Model to Build Trust HO*. The path of being, first, Beginner, then, Intermediate, then, Advanced, and then, Expert in some task, sport, job, specialty, or trade. Don't let them stay halfway. Teach them to delay the reward, realizing that when they wait, it is increased many times over.

To your students: see to it that their grades and your feedback have a straight, honest, and useful purpose. It's not about you, it's about them: your student. Give them the medal only if they deserve it, don't give it to them if they don't deserve it. You will corrupt others and the education system if you fail to give correct and trustworthy recognition. It is one of those failures that cause general contamination. It spreads like the *Coronavirus*; everyone will want the same kind of favorable recognition for poor results. It recommends the path of correction or overcoming. Don't show acceptance for a level of comfort, convenience, and low performance. Be a provider of knowledge, but also of self-improvement, objective and fair treatment with qualifications and practical application of knowledge.

To your neighbors: take care, first of all, not to cause them any inconvenience, and if there is any, for any party, noise, or construction you carry out, anticipate warning them and agree on give-and-take agreements. It lubricates the human relationship, because you don't know when you will be a provider and when you will be a client of your neighbor. A good sidewalk, a good tree, a good entrance, can give you comfort and, in that sense, welcome and be a client of your neighbor; perhaps unintentionally, but a neglected entrance is to be a bad provider for the neighbors and, above all, something that detracts from the value of the property and the neighborhood. After lubricating the relationship with your neighbors, providing some of the community's own satisfiers that are useful to you and the neighborhood, participate in the improvement of your neighborhood. Make, for a while, clients to your community; without being paid, be a provider of improvements to your neighborhood. The benefits to your neighborhood benefit you.

To your classmates: take care of doing something to achieve a benefit for all, participating in obtaining additional benefits to the study, such as events of improvement, of healthy coexistence, of adding value for new knowledge or new experiences useful to all. Be a provider of generation improvements. Do not be a client of initiatives that harm the generation, much less a provider of them.

To your neighbor in distress: take it upon yourself, when you can, to be a free provider of some support. Being a free provider, you have no obligation other than to do good, do no harm and only give what you decide. Beneficiaries can be your best teachers, get closer.

To your workers/collaborators: take care, first, of the fulfillment of the agreements with religiosity, and extend a friendship with each one of them, without Conflict of Interest. Be a demanding but Trustworthy client of the results of their work and be a provider of the services that you represent and committed to give them with Trustability in your role as a boss.

To your colleagues at work: first, the best teamwork starts with doing your individual work flawlessly and leading by example. Second, extend your work to make your partner's job easier and more comfortable, but don't let them give up on what they must do. Third, do not criticize the work of others, for reasons of seeking personal power and without having a proposed solution, but only when appropriate, so that your contribution is productive, and your criticism is trustworthy. Be a provider of a work environment that is positive, enriching, and full of positive emotions.

To the government of your municipality, your state, and the federal government: *Render unto Caesar the things that are Caesar's and unto God the things that are God's.* Be a trustworthy provider in the payment of your taxes and demands; in other words, be a demanding client in government services to the community. It contributes to the common good, since there is no budget that can meet all the needs of the community.

To your adversary or competitor: on the field, surpass them with better qualities and results. Remember, it is best to win by a lot, because winning by a little is doubtful and in some cultures, it is more difficult to recognize the result. Example: in boxing, when there is a tie, the champion wins, which means that to dethrone a champion there must be a notorious difference. With the rules of the game, be respectful and obedient. Off the field, cultivate respect and chivalry first: *politeness does not take away from bravery*; it cultivates events of improvement for the good of the sector, of the trade, because it benefits both; it cultivates friendship. In many cases, they can complement each other and can be recommended to clients, depending on their different approaches. Be a client or be a provider of your competitor in transparent, productive, and trustworthy agreements. Sportsmanship is what is trustworthy, it is a great value, and that great value is sometimes absent to the detriment of all.

To your suppliers: with these recommendations, you will be able to handle them very well, because you will be balanced by being a demanding but empathetic customer, because you know how to be a good supplier.

And in all cases, watch how your neighbor responds when you make them your customer, whether formally or informally; watch what happens after you deliver a product or service to your customer; watch the production chain; watch what happens to what you delivered: see what happens. This is the connection that we will talk about later in the next *Factor 7: Connection,* of this *Model to Build Trust HO*.

These responses from your neighbor teach you more than all the classes you've ever had; it's the *university of life*. You will find wrong perceptions and right perceptions of them to the same product or service. You will find different reactions, some favorable and some not; you will observe negative and positive emotions. They help you a lot to adapt to the next time you interact with them. They help you for objectivity, humility, and prudence. You will find what is objective; what is yours, which is subjective; what is subjective of the satisfied client; what is subjective of the dissatisfied client.

If you find that a virtuous circle is generated or that you have generated a virtuous circle, there is synergy and benefit. If you find that a vicious circle was formed, with what you delivered or with what resulted in the production chain, you must analyze the causes. That launches you in the process, in the sport of jumping over obstacles, which is a practice that you must learn and develop all your life.

See if your client is Trustworthy or Untrustworthy, to give value to their reactions. Give weight to the remarks of the Trustworthy client, don't give weight to the remarks of the Untrustworthy client. Solving a problem that is not a problem is a very common trap that you must learn to avoid, which happens when you listen to untrustworthy people. Getting to the root cause, not just addressing symptoms, nor *fake* or unreliable information, helps you.

If the chain results in common good, you are a *co-creator* of well-being. Continue to the extent of your possibilities and resources. Acceptance is given in tangible form, generating orders, or requiring your time.

If the results of your product or service led to harm, as opposed to benefit, stop your sourcing. Don't be a *co-creator* of damage. You can correct or you can suspend, and make it clear, that the reasons, is to cause Trustability, in providing common good, useful.

ASSISTANCE TECHNIQUES: Client Assessments; Voice of the Client; NPS Clients; Client Mapping; Client Satisfaction Opportunity Area Identification Groups; Focus Groups; Market Intelligence; Client Recognition.

F7.   CONNECTION

It requires going beyond the specialized work you do.

It is required to connect with 2 dimensions:

1. With the complete production chain, to know the adaptation you need to make in your specialty, given the particularities of your production sector.

2. Connect your technical competencies *(hard skills)* of your trade or career, with your sensitive people *skills (soft skills)*, with Emotional Intelligence to assemble your specialty, with others and with your internal and external clients.

It is required to connect with the entire chain of jobs, all the way to the end client. The question must be answered: For what and for whom am I doing what I am doing, and after answering the question, ask yourself again: For what and for whom and what follows, until the end of the chain is reached: What is the final product resulting from the chain? This allows you to feel and see your contribution in the final result of the chain and, in addition, gives meaning to what you do. I am referring to following the chain of activity and the objective that is met by each link in the chain of activities.

This is how a Trustworthy chain of events is established, and not that only one of the links is Trustworthy. This is how the chain of productive interrelation and reliability is established. This is how a trustworthy organization is established because a common final objective is pursued, and everyone must do well the link that corresponds to them in the production chain, in addition to collaborating with the other links, to achieve together the overall final objective.

It is also very important to have and recognize shared merit, in addition to individual merit. An example of the above is that of a bricklayer working in a cathedral who, when asked what his work consisted of, replied: *in bringing people closer to God*. The worker lays bricks, but realizes the whole chain, and perceives and feels that it is to bring people closer to God, so it makes a lot of sense to him to be able to contribute.

Specialization allows you to go deeper into a field and concentrate on it, but it often happens that the proper solution lies between two specialties; that is, in the middle of the two, or else, you need to know about both. In Construction, it happens between the Architecture specialty and the Civil Engineering specialty. Another example is between the specialty of traumatology and neurology, in matters of the spine, which has bones, ligaments and electric wiring, that is, nerves. It also happens between strategic planning and marketing in business.

Connection, then, is very important to master the entire chain; if possible, mastering each specialty, but often, knowing who to consult, who to buy from and who to delegate to.

Also, it is necessary to be connected between what is the domain of specialties, which is called: *hard skills*, with the part of dominating sensitivity, achieving consensus with people, *win-win* negotiation, delegating achieving successful results, which is called *soft skills,* and also, being connected with Ethics and honesty to be able to achieve trustworthy results.

Hard skills, *soft skills*, and *Ethics*: three ideal pillars in the structure to be Trustworthy. Remove one of these pillars and there is no Trustability.

It is another way of expressing what we have already written, that is, to be Trustworthy, it is required to be Ethical and to be Competent and, deploying being competent, it turns out to be competent-rational and analytical in what you do, for what you know, and to be competent-intuitive and sensitive to whom you do it. It is not the same to serve a child, an adult, an elderly person, a sick person, a healthy person, a person in a vulnerable situation, a person in power, a company, a government, a housewife, a lawyer, a doctor, or an engineer. Know your client to serve them better.

In management positions, it is essential to have both parts in good shape, both to have *hard skills*, of the specialty you manage, at least master the *hard skills* of a strong specialty, which makes you understand and feel what you manage, and to have *softs skills* to deal with people. Both are essential to the position of chief. We go deeper into this when we talk about *Institutional Leadership*, in *Factor 3* of the *Model to Build Trust HO*.

An example can be seen in the behavior of this pandemic, comparing Japanese culture and the culture of many other countries.

The Japanese have been using masks since before the pandemic, because those who already have the flu use them to avoid infecting others. Thinking of others, in the first instance, and deciding by conscience and Emotional Intelligence, the action of covering the mouth, with all the discomfort it causes, even if the person does not feel directly benefited by the mouth cover, because the flu already has it, and that does not mean it will go away.

Whereas, in other cultures, most people think that using the mask is to avoid infecting themselves, so that, when they already have the virus, they consider it unnecessary to cover their mouths, and say, "What are they covering themselves for?

ASSISTANCE TECHNIQUES: Process Mapping; Emotional Intelligence at Work; Leadership.

F8. PLANNING BEFORE EXECUTING

Study, planning, and preparation are required prior to execution. To have a sufficiently complete plan, before executing. Sometimes, as you go along, you overcorrect. This carries additional costs. This is noticeable during execution, where there are many improvisations and deviations from the original budget. It has been proven that, if you dedicate more effective time to Planning, even if it costs more, you will save more, since planning generates a smoother and more efficient execution that decreases the total cost.

Another aspect related to this point is prevention rather than reaction when the problem has already occurred. When investing in an asset, the cost of maintenance and the problems that the asset will entail are often overlooked. This is such a terrible lack of foresight that it could doom such an investment to failure. It is very important, at this point, to learn to analyze, project scenarios, diagnose, prioritize, make decisions, reach consensus, and manage in a more complete way.

The only thing that is correct, from a Trustability point of view, is that the job is paid for doing the job well, not just for doing the job. The 3 performance components are on time, within the agreed cost and with the specified quality and guarantees. Planning allows you to foresee in advance to solve those execution details, which are defects, failures, rework, incidents and, of course, accidents.

Valuable time of many people, mistakes and a lot of reworks would be saved by planning what is to be done, say, the day before and half an hour before starting the job. In addition, if the work is a team effort, that half hour of team planning is urgently needed to reach an agreement before doing the day's work.

ASSISTANCE TECHNIQUES: Effective Management of Meetings; Personal Planning of Professional Work; Follow-up on Critical Work Items.

F9. DEPLOY, STREAMLINE, AND CONTROL INPUTS

A very important part of planning is to assemble what is done in-house with what is done through third parties or suppliers. There is a culture of blaming others and suppliers become a focus of blame. Blame others. *It was not me.* It is a social cancer.

It is necessary to take the responsibility of *YES, WE CAN* and, for that, to take the responsibility of preparing yourself with all the inputs, tools, and equipment to be able to do your job.

It's very easy to say, *I was ready, but the provider of the equipment, or the tools, or the person responsible for bringing this or that, wasn't ready.* Here it is necessary to absorb the work of planning in advance those inputs, tools, and equipment, ensuring with time and detailed follow-up, the availability as a proper function.

It is required to display in black and white, the inputs, tools, and equipment necessary to perform the task, and to optimize the detail processes contributing to the success of the task. This is the difference between working with quality and Trustability or not. Mastering and being able to improve *the detail of the detail*, of how to do what is done, is to work with quality and trustability.

It's the difference between being serious about what you do and doing it on the *fly*. Picture a concert pianist, a top-level dancer, a B-787 pilot, an open-heart surgeon, a Formula 1 car racer; they, as a matter of course, master the *detail of the detail* of their intervention, otherwise they fail. Well, I wonder: Shouldn't it be the same with other professions, engineers, lawyers, businessmen, politicians, and civil servants doing their jobs?

Why shouldn't they be equally responsible, if both strongly affect one' s personal life and the lives of others?

There are 2 ways of working:

1. I try to start the execution, without having the proper tools, nor the mental preparation necessary for a quality execution.
2. Before I start to execute, I make sure I have all the tools and materials I need and, in addition, a plan of the work I am going to do. I already have control of everything, what is generally needed in my specialty, and I apply *Pareto's law*, to already have planned and available what is needed most of the time and save the time to see what I need to bring and buy.

Point 2 is the process that gives Trustability.

A person and a process are Trustworthy when you make your provider Trustworthy. Developing Trustworthy suppliers is part of the *Model to Build Trust HO.*

When it comes to assembling something purchased and using blueprints, the first thing to explain, especially, is the layout of everything you need to have before proceeding to assemble: the clear identification and layout of each component.

Another way to interact with suppliers in a trustworthy way is to integrate them very well into your production chain. That is, in the event that your provider's technology is very complex, and it is not easy for you to master it in order to add it to your company, or the investment required to make this integration is beyond your reach.

In the automotive industry, its strategic suppliers are on the same production line, working side by side for the client, which is the automaker.

ASSISTANCE TECHNIQUES: Provider Development; Strategic and Efficient Procurement; *Pareto Law*; ERP; Provider Evaluation; Supply Chain; Logistics; Provider and Contractor Supervision.

F10. EXECUTION AND TESTING

Work with efficiency, productivity, and quality, knowing in advance that your work and that of others will be measured in time, compliance, quality, and cost.

The moment of truth is when you are faced with a task that must be accomplished in a certain time frame, with a commitment, whether personal or agreed upon.

F10.1. Four Worlds in Execution

In *Factor 2: Commitment/Organized Willingness*, we talk about 4 different Worlds: the first, the Execution itself; the second, the bosses, *coaches*; the third, the *staff*; the fourth, the judges.

The execution of the corresponding tasks in each of these 4 Worlds is different. The way they think about the correct execution of their tasks is also different.

Conflicts come when a way of thinking that is good for one World is confused but is applied in another of those Worlds. Trustability is lost. For example, giving a strong order in World 3, bypassing an internal client in World 2, is not very trustworthy.

In moments of truth, it is the World of execution, especially World 1 (the so-called *line*), that is the priority. The one who plays the leading role is always World 1.

Therefore, it is important to give this priority in this factor to World 1, the World of the *line*, in its execution.

Those who belong to the other 3 Worlds must give the importance and recognition to the members of World 1, so that, in the moments of truth, there will be success.

It is to this World 1 that I will now refer.

World 2, of giving direction, guidance, and leadership, I covered this in *Factor 3: Institutional Leadership,* of this *Model to Build Trust HO*.

World 3, of the *Staff* and World 4, of the Judges, are covered in this section, at the end.

F10.2. Basic objectives to be achieved in World 1 of the Execution

- Standardize and homogenize best practice.
- Zero failures.
- Get it right the first time.
- Zero accidents.
- Compliance within the agreed time.

F10.3. Thinking, Feeling, Acting and Checking

Thinking in order to act, we had said, is different from thinking in order to think or reflect or thinking in order to speak or say.

In the execution of the work it is a matter of actively thinking to act, to perform, to do it correctly, without fail. Facts, achievements, actions, decisions, realities. Concentration on the moment and conditioning on tasks is crucial.

The neural group of the mind that is in charge of launching the execution, is more connected with the muscles, to do, to perform something with the hands, arms, legs, feet, and the rest of the body, than the neural group of thoughts, the one in charge of speaking or reflecting.

In the execution of tasks, you must be physically conditioned for the job.

Conditioned means that your body must have a well-adapted routine to perform the precise, necessary movements. It is your body and the cellular memory of your body's muscles that plays the major role in task performance. This demands Practice and Flight Hours to effectively perform the tasks.

And when the task is delicate, it carries risks of accidents; it becomes, then, more critical. Risks to oneself is one thing, and risks to third parties make it even more delicate and critical.

Concentration on today, on the task, in such a way that all 5 senses are on the same thing, well-conditioned and synchronized, is crucial.

When it comes to this approach to execution, the mind cannot be distracted by other mental tasks of criticism, speculation, reflection, new things of disruption. In this world of execution, you can't be *multitask* at any given time, because you make mistakes. *You are either in or you are not.* If you *are not there* at the precise second, the task will not go well. *To be,* means, with all your senses and synchronized with your *target*, with your objective. Unity between your purpose, intention, focused thinking, conditioned body, precise realization in every microsecond and union with your objective to have a good result. There is no other option. You realize the whole cycle of your performance, successes, failures; and when you become perfect in your doing, you feel self-sufficient and complete in a cycle of your life. It is a magical and universal feedback. You feel the realization, you receive information about yourself from the universe.

I imagine that this is what the eagle feels when it flies and undertakes a maneuver, dives, and picks up its food, let's say, from the sea, with precision; when the squirrel flies, jumping from one tree to another; when the dolphin swims and comes out of the water with a pirouette and its entry into the water is impeccable. It feels, I *did the right thing,* and the result is a consequence of what I did. Thank you for having achieved the desired result, or, if the result was not what I expected, then I have to learn more because I could not, maybe a little of both, because I only achieved part of what I wanted. Magical feedback from the universe. I search, I realize, and I find.

In this world of execution, the urgent takes priority over the important. Delivering on time is more important than inventing a better method.

Not all managers understand this need for concentration and non-distraction, nor do all executors. A great disservice is done when the mentality that erroneously prevails in the World of *doing* (World 1), is thinking to criticize, thinking to speculate, and thinking to philosophize, politicize and talk. When this happens, then, acting and decisions to act are inhibited, and passivity comes to rule the World of *doing*. Serious crisis. Tangents emerge that seek to replace good work with good speech. For example: wanting to see the business in the courts, in politics, instead of free competition, demonstrating with facts the worth of the product or service for its inherent value (design, reliability, delivery, useful usability, warranty, patent, price). In this crisis, nobody does, nobody performs, because nobody wants to make mistakes in order not to be criticized and belittled. Such are bureaucratic organizations governed by ideological or political interest. It is also when the sportscaster, who is supposed to be very intelligent, criticizes sportsmen, but does not know how to direct them; it is also when the bullfighting commentator shows that he knows more than the bullfighter, but does not dare to take part in the bullfight.

As I mentioned before, the emotional disposition to face these tasks is very important, because as good chefs say: *if you are in a bad mood or in emotional conflict, emotionally indisposed, distracted, or distressed, the dish comes out and tastes bad*. So says the airline pilot, *if you are in serious emotional conflict, don't fly*.

Hard skills and *soft skills* are necessary for the performance of these execution tasks; *sound mind, sound body*, with a peaceful spirit. In order to achieve concentration, you have to overcome your inner enemy, which is distraction, on the one hand, and adversity, on the other. You are between a rock and a hard place.

F10.4. *HO Method* to achieve Excellence Objectives

Achieving what you do well is not just a matter of doing it and that's it, but that by doing it, you can aspire to excellence. You need to be an expert in what you do.

Being an expert in what you do doesn't come for free or quickly. It costs sacrifice, because it generally forces you to perform activities that are heavy, physically, or emotionally. If the body is not ready, it has to be conditioned, and it costs.

In addition, you have to know, to do.

In the physical and natural world, it is explained by the example of: *Don't climb the tree if you don't know how to get down*. Even if you don't need to know how to get off at first, you will need to know how to get off later, and if you don't, you will be in big trouble when the time comes.

Apply this to any specialty or trade.

When you dedicate yourself to a trade, you live from it and other people depend on your trade: it is irresponsible not to become an expert.

The ethical thing is to be Trustworthy, and to be Trustworthy, you need to be an expert in your core business. Even if you don't like some things, they have to be done, for example, checking.

1. First, go through the entire process with the mind. Example: track competitors first walk the track, and mentally master it.

2. Identify the effort, energy, concentration, and skill requirements for each part of the entire process. This is anticipating potential problems and solving them earlier.

3. Identify possible risks that could lead you to fail to meet the objectives outlined in Item 2, basic objectives to be achieved in World 1, of the Execution. This is to anticipate possible problems and solve them mentally before they arise.

4. Rate risks according to frequency and severity. This is very important to master the process, and not to let the process master you. Identify what the risks are and also identify the severity of each of those risks. Then, identify, for each of these risks, the frequency with which they occur. Experiment on someone else's head, knowing what happens to others who execute this process. There is always history in these activities. The activities that have no history are those of innovation, and we will see those in *Factor 15: Continuous Improvement and Innovation* of the *Model to Build Trust HO*.

5. You have to apply *Pareto's Law and* concentrate on those serious risks and those frequent risks to see how you are going to avoid them.

6. Focus on how the execution should be to avoid those risks; how you should reinforce your concentration, your skills, or your support team for it.

7. Try it until you master it*(Trial and error)*.

8. Perform the complete execution, through the normal learning curve process, noting and measuring the 4 levels of mastery:

1- Beginner.

2- Intermediate.

3- Advanced.

4- Expert and Master.

First, as a Beginner, do it with help or supervision.

Second, as an Intermediate, progressing through the easier parts of the entire process until they are mastered.

Third, as Advanced, master the more difficult stages and activities.

Finally, as an Expert, act without supervision, and you can now supervise and teach the whole process and its parts to others.

Performing this *HO Method* teaches you to live life. Because life is a journey of perfection, learning to improve and become more competent in being useful, in creating value.

This *HO Method* gives you mastery over material things; but, in obtaining that mastery, it forces you to have humility, to recognize your limitations and to have to pay a price. Humility serves you for your life and to be Trustworthy.

It is the best education you can give your children. It teaches you that first, it is to take good care of yourself and then comes happiness in the form of inner satisfaction. Happiness comes as a consequence.

It teaches you to achieve something worthwhile, but which requires effort and sacrifice, which is what gives you greater satisfaction than immediate pleasures, without any process of perfection, which generate a feeling of insatiability.

Postponing gratification is indispensable to be able to do a good job, well done, well proven.

Your body tends to the easy way, to comfort always and, on the other hand, the work, many times, demands activities that do not conform to what is that comfort. Here it is working against the current and natural inertia, at first. Sacrifice? Well, yes, and effort, too. However, the body, by forcing it for good, comes to adapt, and you create a new level of comfort that is more satisfying.

Challenging your body to new levels of adaptation is the norm for every Confident person. When value is created, it pays off.

F10.5. Fields of Emotional Intelligence

Emotional Intelligence points out 4 basic fields:

The first Field is to be able to get along well with others, because you can get along well with yourself, you understand and manage your emotions well and you can understand the emotions of others.

The second field is to focus on your own, with objectivity, impulse control, and pressure tolerance, without getting out of your mind, without losing emotional control, flowing towards your goal, with emotional stability.

The third Field is to inspire others and attract them like a magnet. Radiate magnetism through your chemistry, your self-confidence, your orientation to see for others and support.

The fourth Field is to flow with the universe in general, in balance, what can be called: spiritual intelligence, placing the context of life with death. The Emotional Intelligence of a higher consciousness, or as they say in the East, *Enlightened*. Buddha or Christ. Where you are no longer vulnerable and where you transcend.

On the subject of Execution, when I speak of a correct emotional disposition, in any of the 4 Worlds specified in *Factor 2: Commitment/Organized Will*, the priority is the second Field of Emotional Intelligence of self-control, to be able to flow yourself with achieving the objective in a stable, efficient, impeccable, and Trustworthy way. Emotional stability is essential because the environment is one of adversity and pressure. This requires CHARACTER, and its formation is slow and based on trial and error.

In World 1, *line*, is more priority this disposition of Character, because at the moment of truth, the business, product, service, matter, game, and concert, depends 100% on them, on the participants of World 1.

In the subject of human profiling, the dosage of the variable Stability, or in other words, Constancy and refinement of details and the use of microseconds over time, is vital; it is what makes the difference in excellent, regular, mediocre, or bad performance.

Being Trustworthy means doing the task well, avoiding and minimizing risks, having planned the result, and achieving it; having prepared and trained many times; being committed with high personal motivation and, if possible, with passion; being happy in and with what you do, as well as having an environment that favors that motivation.

The greatest reward for those who love their work, in World 1, where there is a lot of execution, is the work itself, because it allows them to be in their World. Where there are cycles that begin, last and end, begin again and are perfected; that make the person be focused and flowing with their mind, body, spirit, and their tangible objective. To get it right requires that connection with the universe, in the here and now, that synchronization in time, of various body movements, synchronization of sight, sound, touch, movement, rhythm, touch, *timing*, with a result, with an outcome, with an achievement, with an end.

When you are busy, focused, that's your World; everything else is left over in those moments. It's you, with your task and your goal and your result. That union of you, with your execution and with your result, is to feel self-sufficient, within that time. It is a time of personal fulfillment.

Cases that illustrate this point very well, is the execution of aviation tasks by the pilot and co-pilot; trailer driving tasks on the road, with dangerous loads; surgery tasks in the operating room, open heart and organ transplants; tasks of hot connection of high voltage cables, in electrical transmission; tasks of counting red blood cells in the laboratory; tasks of playing, singing or dancing at a concert; task of racing as a Formula 1 or motorcycle driver during the race, sports tournaments and Olympics.

But also sweeping, cleaning, housekeeping, cooking, laying bricks, sowing, cutting firewood, harvesting, bookkeeping, carpentry, mechanics, welder, electrician, production operator, press, lathe, milling machine, cutter, unit control machines and assembly, are execution tasks, which require high concentration and belong to this World 1.

F10.6. Exercise your Freedom by choosing your Vocation

This World of execution is so important that, to be able to do well these tasks of each trade, of each specialization, requires so much time and dedication, that it takes your life. There is so much mental and physical conditioning to do it well and reduce the risk of failure that it is not possible for human beings to master many specialties during their lifetime of, say, a hundred years, because they do not have the time necessary to master them and perform them well. Time is short. You do one or the other, but you can't do too many. In addition, there are some that conflict with each other in certain respects. For example, there is no one who could have been a champion boxer, a good concert violinist, a champion Formula 1 race car driver, and a good surgeon at the same time. It is almost impossible, as there is not enough time in life to acquire the skills and the physical and mental conditioning to master these specialties.

It is necessary to choose, in order to do well, what has to be done. It is when you exercise your own freedom; choose, you can't do everything. Character is required. It is necessary to educate in freedom, to choose among many things. In choosing your vocation and your devotion, in placing yourself in the context of total and real life, of death (Fourth Field of Emotional Intelligence: placing yourself in the context of life and death, your own life and family life).

But whatever you choose, do it in a Trustworthy way, otherwise, it would be betraying your own selection of what you chose, and your body will understand it as incongruity. And the incongruity is noticeable, sickening.

Within this World of stability and the search for perfection, one must avoid the neurosis for perfection in the World of Execution, which can also be an inner enemy. The Fourth

Field mentioned in Emotional Intelligence, that of placing yourself in the universal context, with a spirit of peace and connection, avoids the neurosis of perfection in your profession. In other words, alienation. And this alienation is avoided when you place the context of life within the space, where there are other things to do and it is convenient to do, choosing, within your freedom and your capacity, according to the cycles of your life, the balance with what your family demands in the different moments of its evolution. This is crucial.

F10.7. Continuity vs. Disruption by innovation

We said that, in this World of Execution, of continuous operation, it is not possible to do, at the same time, the precision of the learned practice (operative underworld) with the creativity of innovating a different one, not yet learned; that is, to do something new (innovative underworld) and the operative continuity, cause problems, cause possible failures.

How to be in the best of the 2 underworlds since both are needed?

- Create a space that does not negatively affect the continuity of the operation with what is already known and, in that space, try new methods and changes.

- Form a team of people with experience and proven Trustability, to innovate and have performance protocols in terms of measurement and limits to act.

- Once, on a pilot basis, value has been demonstrated, then introduce into the line of operations through an application of an experience curve.

In such a way that the company continues with:

- Doing what you do right the first time on repetitive tasks, and what you don't, is recorded as rework.
- Innovate and update by means of protocols that combine well to avoid a disruption of the client service and the well-done of the previous point (for example, when repairs are made on roads, and deviations are made so well done, that they do not cause any inconvenience to *clients-users-drivers-passengers*).
- Introduce innovation to the operation with Trustability, and by managing the experience curve, selecting a focused start-up field, and to the extent of its performance, extending it.
- Get it into the zero-failure lane and get it right the first time.

There are many ways to fill this creative space, depending on the complexity of the product, service, or process to be innovated, re-engineered or updated.

First, understand the steps and protocols required to innovate.

To innovate is not just to have ideas and that's it. This is petty, speculative, anecdotal, when it is not accompanied by the process to take that creativity to its realization or implementation.

The more in-depth Innovation part and its concepts will be discussed later in *Factor 15: Continuous Improvement and Innovation*.

F10.8. Verification

There are 3 first instance means of proof of execution:

1. While executing.
2. Final report of the event, shift, game, with appropriate performance parameters.
3. External evaluation report of the final result.

All 3 means are very important to achieve Trustability.

While executing, the executor himself feels and perceives if it was successful or not and can correct it during the course of the event.

The final report of the event or shift or game must be made at the end of the day.

Some examples of reports are as follows

- In aviation: at 11:00 pm, daily, when the last flight of the day arrives and lands, an immediate tally is made of how the punctuality of all flights was; what the percentage of flight occupancy was; incidents that occurred that did not lead to accidents, and accidents (if any), or if not, the good message of zero accidents; equipment failures on time, as a percentage of uptime, or if not, the good message of zero equipment failures. It is a daily comparison between actual performance and target objectives.

- In production: at the end of the shift, total kilograms produced in kilograms with first-rate quality and total kilograms produced with second-rate quality; wastage as a percentage of production; quality of raw materials received; direct cost incurred versus direct cost budgeted; on-time and off-time deliveries to customers; punctuality and attendance of the work team; downtime due to equipment failure; overtime; rework; accidents occurred. It is a shift-by-shift comparison between actual performance and target objectives.

- In a basketball game: *final score*; percentage of baskets scored, out of total shots; rebounds obtained for and against; steals for and against; percentage of points from free throws scored; assists for and assists missed; injuries; sports incidents.

- In personal work: attempts made vs. successes achieved; failures incurred as a percentage of total performance; percentage of time in optimal energy conditions vs. percentage of time in low energy conditions.

Regarding the third-party evaluation report, it is important to note that this report may come from several sources:

- From the client.
- From users.
- As witnesses or spectators.
- From experts or commentators or press.
- From the *coach* or technicians of the team.
- From the competitors.

Each of these audiences provides information from its own perspective and, therefore, this information should be taken relatively to those perspectives.

The message, with these evaluations, is that we are in a glass house, and that leads us to always be willing to face the truth; our actions are noticed, just as our body notices our congruencies or incongruencies, and to understand the different sieves of truth, according to different perspectives.

In fact, your own mind yields different perspectives, depending on which neural cluster is active. If the logical thinking neural group is more active, it tells you about the chronology of the event and time management. If the one who is active is the visionary, it gives you the perspective of what should be or what could have been. If the one that is active is the analytical one, it tells you about the failures incurred and the causes of those failures. If the intuitive is active, it tells you who and what mood the people involved in the event are in.

Which perspective is the true one?

The thesis of this book is that Trustworthy people and organizations take the 4 perspectives, they take the perspectives of the different participants: the optimists, the pessimists, and the centered ones, only as a reference to use them to make their own final diagnosis, and that is how they are able to catapult themselves to be better. On the contrary, those who take only their unique perspective, and make it their law, are unreliable people and organizations that sooner or later fail.

Generally, in very sophisticated companies in their administration, they make reports with the Trustability approach, being that this mentality should be created and instilled, even in a simple and incipient way, in all actions, whether of companies or individuals. We have to create a culture of keeping it simple. For example, in the sport of baseball, it is very numerical and people who practice and like this sport, automatically receive this habit of measuring performance, and it is very easy and natural for them to transport this culture to their work and family life *(score*, runs for and runs against, in 9 episodes). 3 *strikes* and 4 balls as batting limits and *fouls* do not count. Pitching, base on balls, single, double, triple or *home run*, as possible batting results.

In fielding 3 *outs*, with errors and hits scored). Children learn it very well. The U.S. culture was very much shaped by baseball, and that's how organized they are at work, and it gives them a Trustability advantage.

F10.9. Execution in World 3, the Staff World

In this World 3, there is the function of administration with its accounting and finance, the function of human capital support, project engineering, production process technology, information technology, legal and juridical support, and reliability assurance.

Thinking for Doing, as well as the above, requires high concentration and practice in each of these functions.

The difference between the people of World 1 and World 3 is that the people of World 3 are not directly responsible for the *score* of the results achieved with the client, of each product or service delivered, and which form the so-called *core business,* the backbone of the business.

So, the execution approach leads us to what to do with your specialty to support a good *score* with the client, without being directly responsible for the *core business,* but for part of the environment that surrounds World 1, which is directly responsible for achieving a good *score*.

What needs to be added in the approach of the participants in this World 3, is the collaboration to give support and support to those in World 1, and the execution of the function to achieve a favorable environment to the business, to the game, to the institution, to the company.

In general, *Thinking for Doing*, in this World 3, does not have a daily operational routine as rigid as in World 1, but rather, the time for the execution of tasks has a little more space and slack to be carried out where there is more opportunity to reflect, propose solutions and different options. More time to analyze, evaluate, and then, make the decision.

It is more difficult to have physical, logical, and tangible measurements in World 3.

Therefore, the results obtained in the management of World 3 are more ambiguous, more ethereal. However, there is a growing tendency to make their measurement and testing more and more precise.

The profile of the participants of this World 3 is a little more thoughtful and less executor, compared to the participants of World 1, as well as more options and diversification of possibilities to move than the participants of World 1.

The recommendation of this book, in World 3, is to focus your tasks on who your internal clients are and treat them with all the methodology mentioned here of the 6 steps to organize the Provider-Client-User interrelationship. This leads them to be more collaborative and effective in performing their role and, in addition, sets an example to the ones in World 1 of how they should serve their customers.

If those in World 1 feel mistreated by those in World 3, there is an organizational incongruity that sooner or later has a negative impact on the production chain up to the end client (here, being the internal client of the *staff*, I am mistreated, that is, with low Trustability, and the company wants me to treat the end client very well, how is that?)

In some places, it is common for those in World 3, without getting their hands dirty, to be the privileged ones, in terms of treatment, status and economic remuneration. A serious mistake is made, because then it becomes a felt organizational incongruity, in which the *core business* players are undervalued, and with them, go directly to the clients, since they are their direct channel. It is an attack against themselves and against the most critical part of the organization: *clients*, the company's raison d'être.

It is also not correct to belittle those of World 3 in the organization, making them have no authority.

It is like in a good family: there is a father and a mother, both have authority, both have an important part of the work to manage and make decisions in harmony, both have a specialty or trade with which to contribute to the common good of the family.

The only correct thing to do is to make explicit the roles of both Worlds, in each case of interaction of moments of truth, and to clarify roles and corresponding authorities, in addition to a lot of teamwork. To value the positions professionally and remunerate according to High Professional Trustability criteria, and not subjective criteria of: *I think, or so I like it, because I am the boss*.

Example: in certain cases, it may be appropriate for the management owner (World 3) to prohibit a transaction with a client for non-payment, lack of authorized credit in the collection exercise. However, before doing so, unilaterally, you must exhaust communication and collection attempts with the commercial executive in charge of serving that client (understanding that in World 1, you have spent a lot of time with that client and do not want to lose them).

Another example: the head of the Human Resources function can prohibit the entry of a person with evidence of drunkenness, alcohol, or drugs, as long as there is an established policy with its corresponding regulations and procedures; but again, working side by side, as a team, with the head of the corresponding area to support them in what needs to be done to replace them. If the boss himself is the one who talks to the person, all the better; of course, advised by Human Resources.

Another example: the Process Technology function holder may prohibit the modification of a critical operating condition formula for technology reasons that affect the product or service, and a dispute may arise between World 3 and World 1. This controversy must be resolved by the head that is common to both, in order to respect the unity of command. The recommendation is that technology people support in an objective and collaborative way in the exercise of creativity, to find better solutions for the product and the client, sharing information of important technological value.

There are many other cases of helping the members of World 1 to do a better job, with the advice and collaboration of World 3, working side by side, and delimiting, with a charter of responsibilities, the different roles classified as follows:

VETO	Chief Executive Officer Responsible for authorizing or vetoing activities, projects, or results.
LINE MANAGER	Initiates and terminates the activity ensuring Trustability
CONSULTING AND SUPPORT	Provides technical support in a specialized aspect of the activity.

BE INFORMED	Witnesses or people who must be informed in order to prepare for action

Teaching teamwork, with different roles, but as clear and understood as in baseball, or with a chart of responsibilities and roles as above, is one of the best ways to achieve Trustability. The two, with different perspectives, converge for a better result. Here is the synergy that is: *1+1 is 3.* When there is value creation, in the exchange of 2 people, 3 become 3, because it is one, it is the other and it is the added value that generates synergy and multiplies. This is a very valuable force that not everyone knows how to explore or understand, let alone use for the greater good.

Each and every one of the above 4 roles must have the premise of collaboration among all of them, since there are always interfaces between roles and spaces that must be filled with good will and collaboration to complete the work cycles. This collaboration is so important that it is what establishes *Factor 1* of this *Model to Build Trust HO*.

F10.10. Execution in World 4, the World of Judges

The performance in this World 4, is the judgment decision on whether or not the action of the actors is valid, whether in World 1, World 2, or World 3, as the case may be.

Inspectors; hired consultants; people from the Treasury and government; umpires in soccer; umpires in baseball; linesmen; referees in boxing; magistrate judges; commercial judges; among others. They rely for authority on authorized laws and regulations, which they, by official appointment, are permitted to enforce.

Thinking to decide based on an objective judgment. It is not a thinking to perform tasks proper to the actors it judges, it is not a thinking to make the work better or worse, but only to judge a result, regardless of the intentions and ways of doing it or having wanted to do it. In order to ensure your Trustability you need to have no Conflicting Interests, not to be a party in order to be a judge.

Thinking to evaluate and thinking to decide an opinion belongs mainly to the world of analytical and logical thinking. They must have such an EQ that they can rise above spectacular emotional feelings and impressions.

Objectivity, verification, and evidence of causes that are concatenated, is fundamental in the thinking, feeling, and acting of the participants of this World 4. The exact action as it was, not invented or imagined, and if possible, it should be filmed and well documented. These are the fundamental ingredients:

- The law and the rules of the game.
- The personal capacity to judge objectively and assertively.
- Without contaminating the decision by feelings and sympathies that detract from the truth.
- Finally, the right EQ disposition to be assertive, without causing, on purpose, human conflicts or hindering protagonism.

If they are wrong in that the people of this World 4, of Judges, have this profile, a very serious damage is done to the Trustability of the Community.

Errors in this World 4, directly affect the Trustability in the whole sector, a whole company, a whole community.

Sold-out or incompetent refereeing, in Soccer, or any sport, destroys the sport.

The sold-out or incompetent arbitration of a political election destroys not only the policy, but the community.

Those who win or lose with these World 4 errors, re-profile, and act on those judges' rulings, and adapt to whatever needs to be done to get a favorable verdict from the judge. They, then, are largely to blame for creating and nurturing a culture of low Trustability, as they induce an alignment of unworthy and fraudulent behaviors.

The fundamental error triggers, in this World 4, are: Lack of Honesty, Ethics and Truth; the basic premise of Trustability; Conflict of Interest; lack of knowledge of the law and regulations; in addition to the lack of sufficient experience, well capitalized.

On the contrary, the good and trustworthy performance of the Judges of World 4 aligns the behaviors of the community to rise and generate valuable human development.

An example in companies is the bidding process for provider tenders. In the exercise of judging the contestants, it is an act that belongs to World 4, and becomes a great social reference for Trustability.

The most powerful engine to boost competitiveness, Trustability, merits and valuable achievements, are well-done bids, where the best bidder wins, where it is explained why it won, not necessarily for being the cheapest, but the one with the best ratio of guarantees and proven Trustability, in relation to its price; there is congruence with the reality felt by the sector that knows the bidders.

Decisions of winners in bids and appointments to senior positions have a much greater impact on the actual culture than the discourse of values, philosophy, and ideologies. Deeds outweigh words, good intentions and promises.

ASSISTANCE TECHNIQUES: classification of degrees of mastery of the trade; technical certification in the trade; charter of responsibilities to identify and clarify roles; *Lean* organizational structures; techniques for failure analysis and decision making; project administration and management; focus on results; thinking strengths.

F11. QUALITY CONTROL

F11.1. Quality Control Approaches

There are 5 major approaches to Quality Control:

1. The traditional focus of Quality Control is on the final inspection of the finished product before it is delivered to the client.

2. The approach of performing inspection, not only at the end, but also at each step of production and at the raw materials.

3. The approach of extending the inspection of the product over a given time where the product is located, tracing its destination.

4. The approach to control the quality of the processes to work and produce the product or services, in terms of Trustability of what is done, both of the operating conditions, equipment, and technical formulations, as well as written procedures, authorized for the realization of labor and brain work.

5. Statistical process control, reducing variations and perfecting the deviation-proof process.

F11.2. Inspection

In the first 3 approaches, the Quality Control Function belongs to World 4, in terms of Organized Commitment, that is, to the World of Judges, giving their evaluation and judgment. Then, the organizational profile of the Quality Control people is, as established in the point of Execution and Verification, corresponding to World 4.

In the case of country organization, in the form of a republic, the equivalent is the Judicial Power, which is in charge of World 4, the World of Judges, the World of objective and impartial evaluation.

Certified third parties, who represent the duty to be, without Conflict of Interest, issue their judgment in an objective manner and master the knowledge of the established rules of the game or of the subject matter.

Standards, specifications, prototypes, laboratory measurements, contracts, testing, are some of the elements that make up this specialty.

In addition, great statistical knowledge to perform inspections, sometimes exhaustively, sometimes selectively, sometimes by different types of statistically valid sampling.

Physical measurements, chemical measurements, electrical conductivity measurements, magnetic measurements; sometimes the product needs to be destroyed, sometimes it is only damaged and sometimes it is not affected, make up this specialty. Odor, taste, appearance, color, smoothness, viscosity, strength, durability, toxicity, purity, parts per million, flammability, are common parameters in this specialty.

Again: perfection is a very common and recommended tendency in this World.

The natural conflict with World 1 participants is: *don't be so strict, because it affects my performance in terms of delivery*. Sometimes, it is a cause of embarrassment and conflict.

Knowledge of the client's needs is very important in establishing the limits of all these multitude of measurement specifications.

The emotional disposition to explain your specialty well is vital to overcome conflicts. It represents the client, and with it, society.

Sometimes, instead of being obsessed with meeting a specification, the product is customized or classified and put into use, with a written warning, that this product has some special flaw or specification, second or third quality, for example, and has a different, specific, authorized, and valid use.

There is also quality control in services. Example: in software programming, there are a series of application tests to demonstrate whether the program is as expected, inefficient or incomplete for what it is to be used for.

As for connection, beyond the specialty, it is convenient to extend the competence of Quality Control of the product or service, to the Quality Control of the process, to go to the causes that produce to be able to be within quality parameters. What it does cause to be within limits and what it causes to go out of limits.

This is a higher degree of development of Quality Control. This knowledge and skill are required when moving to the Process Quality Control approach, which we will discuss later.

The other strategic aspect of this specialty is the opinion, when there are differences with the final client, where the final client claims that there is poor quality. The linchpin of the balance must be the objective measurement of specifications and the credibility of the Quality Control person, their degree of *expertise* and their correct emotional disposition.

The reliability of the company depends on the excellence of this Quality Control function, which is exemplary and recognized by clients with high credibility.

When clients have confidence in the judgment of these specialists, a Conflict-of-Interest decision, between provider and client, can be resolved through objectivity and truth, and that is when the highest level of performance of this specialty is reached. Recognition of a person with an exceptional expert vocation. For this, many Flight Hours, and a lot of depth of knowledge above others are required.

Under the point of view of Trustability, there are different kinds of experts, and giving recognition to the best of all is very important in the culture of Trustability and the motivation of others to follow their path and example.

F11.3. Process Control

Regarding approaches 4 and 5, which have to do with Process Quality Control, this is a different subspecialty. This requires not only making evaluative judgments of a product or service under certain conditions, but also knowledge of the deep *know-how* to produce or elaborate the service in question, which has to do with the design of the processes themselves.

Chemical, mechanical, electrical, magnetic, mechatronics, hydraulics, energy technology, which has to do with technology and deep engineering. When the complexity of the processes and equipment is high and requires a lot of depth of knowledge, it is recommended that there is a Process Technology function to support the operation.

In the metal-mechanical and automotive sector, it is called: Manufacturing Technology.

Being responsible for process changes and establishing the process conditions under which the operation must function is an activity belonging to World 3, the *Staff* World, and works side by side with the participants of World 1, the Operation.

When there are failures in the operation, sometimes, they are due to errors in the operation itself, but many times, it is due to process and equipment conditions. It is very important to differentiate the cause so that these failures do not recur and are solved at the root. Teamwork and problem-solving spaces to work together, between Process Technology World 3 and Operation World 1, is the right solution for the company. Interdisciplinary *staff/line* teams are often the solution to organizational conflicts and, with it, the increase of Trustability. In this way, avoid differences of personal pride between the heads of one area and another, and change it for the joint pride of belonging to a trustworthy and successful company.

What happens is that there is a natural conflict of perspectives, because one perspective is the solution to resolve a symptom; another perspective is to resolve a different symptom; and another is to resolve a cause of the symptoms. While they agree, there are management and decision-making conflicts, which often result in human conflicts.

The maximum degree of development of this Process Technology specialty is to be able to master not only the *know-how*, but to master the *know why*.

Germany, England, Israel, France, the United States and Japan are countries that have excelled in the invention of technology and are the ones with the highest number of patents, as they are more oriented to technological and scientific research and development. Talking about the connection of going beyond the specialty, here is the border with the research and development function, where there is a clear objective, to discover new ways of doing things better. Develop *know how* and *know why*.

F11.4. Quality as a *Staff* Function

Since the Quality Control and Testing function is very important in Trustability, this function has been extended to all the processes of the company, not only to the technical and operative ones, but also to the administrative and human ones. This extension has been called Total Quality.

Total Quality has 3 fundamental pivots:

- Client satisfaction.
- Quality control in all processes, products, and services.
- The dynamic of continuously improving the above pivots, in a deliberate, orderly, professional, and organized manner, throughout the company or institution, with proven and professional methods.

It is highly advisable to institute the Quality function within World 3, the Staff World, to the operation, where it concentrates on these 3 pivots mentioned here, and to facilitate the ways of working and the methodology, so that each area is responsible for the quality of its processes, but with the help and the methodology of the Total Quality support function.

SUPPORT TECHNIQUES: Quality Manuals; Process Control; Statistics for Quality Control; Interdisciplinary Work Teams; Organizational Development; Black belts; Client Satisfaction Surveys; NPS; Market Intelligence.

F12. EXCELLENCE IN BUSINESS CONTINUITY

In World 1, something very distinctive, is that daily continuity of having to perform repetitive activities, as the scale by volume represents a key advantage to be more productive.

In the 21st century, with the advent of Artificial Intelligence, the first *target* of *AI* is, precisely, to automate repetitive tasks and those well-known and documented by its history: warehousing, transportation, operations, maintenance, online ordering systems, accounting administration, etc., are already automated.

The world will continue to make strong progress in automation.

However, in all those operations that remain to be automated, of which there are many, there must be a focus on avoiding errors, avoiding people's boredom, keeping people's health and energy, and not wasting time.

Even in automated processes, they have to be monitored to be within control limits and people will have to do that operational work, controlling the World 1 machines, managing the changes.

It is required to manage time with professional zeal, *not leaving for tomorrow what can be done today*, understanding time as the most valuable resource, and anticipating problems. Always arriving on time, being punctual, respecting the time of others.

Sense of urgency in time management, doing things with continuity and precision, *more haste, less speed*. You arrive more safely and on time, with a steady but constant speed than with starts and braking.

The enemy is distraction, on the one hand, and boredom, on the other. Both cause problems for the operation. To do this better, it is necessary to discover those details that occur in repetitive operations, but which are subtly different, from one cycle to another cycle of the operation, from one day to the next and, above all, when there are incidents, accidents, or changes. These small details are what lead you to perform well in the middle of these two dangerous extremes. These fine details can only be found and mastered when you are between these two extremes, and they are the ones that tell you loud and clear whether or not you are being Trustworthy, especially if there is an emergency.

For example: in a complex dance, to be able to change rhythm in an instant, or to recover from a mistake, despite inertia, is to demonstrate reliability and *expertise*. In aviation, a change of route, change of traffic decision due to bad weather or other type of emergency, for example, in a landing, when you have to take to the air again, is where there is a difference between experts and non-experts. In the operation of a high-speed weaving machine, when a knot forms outside the norm, and you have to go in to untangle it, either by deciding to stop or by deciding to correct on the fly. In car driving when someone runs a red light and it's your turn to dodge. In these examples, the subtle details are the microseconds that must be used to make the change, and for that, in advance, the expert already knows how to do it, what it feels like and what to do, because he has already done it and it is not so much of a surprise. For them, it's just part of normal operation. Those who do not handle these details will fail more in the change and in the emergency. For experts, in one microsecond, one can make, say, three movements, and for non-experts, only one or none. Those moves are what make the difference between getting ahead or being left out, with all its consequences.

The physiology of our bodies and the connection of the brain, including the muscles and organs, make the difference, because the internalization of movements in an automatic way, is only achieved after much practice and discipline. It is very important that there are 2 personal strategies to achieve this expert conditioning:

1. At first, pay attention, mind, and concentration, on the object of interest, at the precise moment that matters, (remember that only a detail, at a given moment) so that, first, there is synchrony with the instruction that makes your brain to your body to act.

2. When there is a lot of practice, the body learns it without requiring the brain, so it becomes automated and conditioned.

I remember the conversation I had with a pilot with 14,000 flight hours, when I asked him how many times he took off and landed between Monterrey and Mexico City in a year, and if he wasn't bored. His response was: *When you love to fly, you realize the many differences that exist and that you appreciate in each flight,* and he mentioned several, but I perceived his way of approaching life, appreciating every detail that, for many, go unnoticed. Each repeated movement is a really new movement, it cannot be the same, because the previous one has already passed, there have already been changes. The different weather, the different time, the different cloud formation, the cargo, the passengers, the traffic, the co-pilot, the route at each moment, the landscape, the behavior of the aircraft in its different functions, the communications with different people in the control tower and, in all of them, being present the sensation of flying.

This is a clear sign of the balance between continuity of operation and happiness when you are passionate and meaningful about what you are doing in your life. You are busy, you are focused, you are flowing between your thinking and your doing, in an environment with a satisfactory outcome.

The formula for being happy and satisfied by being productive. I take care first, and then, I get satisfaction and happiness from what I get, from what I do. I get a lot of things, not just money. It is the formula that is recommended in times of worry, dissatisfaction, and fear. Get busy and you'll have a better time than thinking, imagining, and letting your mind do its thing. When you are busy, you focus your mind on what you are doing and, if your doing is healthy, useful, and productive, this cures you of mental disorders.

Of course, this formula also applies to non-repetitive and non-operational work, but where you are focusing your mind on something useful and concentrated. What happens is that, with repetitive work, where you combine mind and body in movement, you flow.

If the universe of the stars is infinite and you cannot fully appreciate it all, because of its immensity, the microscopic world of the earth, the plants, the leaf, the cell, the atom, the electron and all the particles found in the *microworld* system, is equally infinite and attractive. The multitude of details that you can appreciate in a field, apparently very small and concentrated, when you go deeper, can also give you the infinity that a larger field of functions and activities gives you.

I remember very well when we awarded the prize of the year, and the cover of the magazine of the company *Celulosa y Derivados, Planta Celofán*, to a worker who succeeded in achieving 20 years without absenteeism and punctuality.

I asked: *How did you do it, didn't you ever get sick?*

The answer was:

> *What happens is that I don't start my work when the shift starts, I start it the day before, before I go to sleep, preparing myself for the next day, physically and emotionally. I did get sick, but thank God, they were not incapacitating illnesses, and sometimes, I went to work a little sick.*

It was then that the idea of combining health and continuous work emerged in my mind. Long life, for those who work orderly and reliably. Busy in body, mind, and soul, serving.

When you find meaning in work, repetitiveness is not a cause for boredom. If you do part of the normal work, avoiding possible negative incidents, accidents, failures and anticipating what is coming, it makes you an expert with a lot of personal satisfaction, and it is a long road of adventure and enormous meaning. If you wrap the work with all the positive consequences that can result, if you do it well, and if you become aware that, to do it, you need to be privileged in health, skills, and energy, it results in gratitude and love. Meaning, gratitude, and love are the cause of a happy life.

You can always manage to create something of additional value in each new operation, in each new cycle, one more detail, one more word, one more fresh smile, one more perfection.

Put your mind where you want to stimulate the detail you want to improve. You are never done and there is always room for improvement. And so you always get better.

Challenges and areas of opportunity are always present:

- Zero failures.
- Zero accidents.
- Zero injuries.
- Zero absences.
- Always maintain a high level of personal energy throughout the day.

There can be no weariness in these pretensions to a high level of excellence.

At the beginning, start with a short time to achieve these *targets,* and then extend the time. First in one day, then in two days, then in a week, then in a month, a year, etc.

In my experience, plants with more than 300 people, working in high-risk processes, have been able to achieve two years of zero accidents, after having a sad history of at least one accident per week.

In the aviation world in the early to mid-1900s, there were a lot of accidents. Today it is the safest means of transport on earth, many times safer than road transport. They set their minds on accidents, on their possible causes and on banishing the causes.

It is important to mention that if such a complex job, such as aviation, can reduce accidents and failures, in less complex jobs, it is imperative that they be corrected; it is not a luxury, it is a social obligation. Failures, errors, and defects seriously affect society, causing problems, high costs and unnecessary sacrifices.

F13. FAULT DETECTION AND LEARNING FROM MISTAKES

It is required to analyze failures and learn from them to improve the way of doing things. This practice generates many solutions to areas of opportunity.

When the bosses punish the person who executes the failures to make it clear that they are not the guilty ones; when they hide the failures so as not to be punished and the executors are covered up; when they let the failures go unnoticed, they incur in low Trustability.

When there is a culture of Trustability, mistakes are excellent raw material for learning. In Michael Jordan's book, he talks about how the map provided by the mistakes he made showed him the route to practice for correction and with it, the clear path to excellence. At the end it states *I am what I am, thanks to my mistakes.*

Human errors are generally due to ignorance or lack of practice*(Pareto's Law)*. Sometimes, however, the error is due to a willful and malicious act. In the latter case, it is useful to look at the cause of this resentment in order to learn to see the root cause (see *Factor 19*): *Development Strategies* and *Factor 20: Human Motivation Strategies)*.

There is an excellent technology to technically analyze and solve failures in repetitive processes, especially:

- Statistics is a fundamental subject.
- The basic mathematics of Quality.
- Decision-making under the *Kepner & Tregoe* method.
- Japanese Quality methods and *Black Belt* technology.
- The theories of the two precursors of Japanese Quality: Joseph Juran and Edward Deming.

The Japanese, guided by Deming and Juran, packaged these tools very well, with the simple, statistical methods of classification, focalization, grouping, frequency of occurrences, homogenization, standardization, localization, *Pareto's Law*, Normal Distribution, and *Ishikawa Diagram*, combined with evaluations of the consequences that yield diagnoses of costs of Non-Quality, extremely useful in the process of Trustability management and in the solution of failures and quality improvement.

The *Kepner & Tregoe* method of decision making is based on the approach of proposing alternative solutions, evaluating them, and making decisions with the different perspectives. In addition to Kepner & Tregoe, the *Human Side* tool, in its Thinking Process Chapter, clearly leaves us with 4 different perspectives that every leader must manage: The perspective of logic in time: the chronology (Logical Thinking); the perspective of causes and not symptoms (Analytical Thinking); the perspective of a long future and the natural evolution of influential events (Visionary Thinking); and the perspective of how it impacts people, and the acceptance or not, of the possible solution (Intuitive Thinking).

Failure chains. It has been found, in the investigation of accidents, both industrial, in manufacturing plants, in construction and in aviation, that behind the accident, there is a series of previous failures, and that almost always, there are warning signs that could have prevented the accident if they had been attended to. This led to the inclusion in reliability management of the continuous identification of incidents or failures. By avoiding incidents and failures, accidents are largely corrected. More than 80% of accidents (Pareto's Law) are due to chains of minor failures that occurred prior to the accident.

The opposite of this Trustability culture of incident and failure management is the culture of blaming an accident on a single cause and closing the case. This is a sign of a culture and an institution of Low Trustability.

To all of the above, we must add the methodology of parallel organization, where quality circles and interdisciplinary team building are used to learn from mistakes in order to solve problems and create a culture of success. Here the new culture is created with 3 new parameters:

1. Critical spirit and openness, to bring to light the failures and problems, but with a strong attitude to solve them, to be an important contributor to the solution. Proactivity demonstrated with deeds, not words.

2. The important thing is to find the failures, their cause, the problem, and not to find the culprits, because these supposed culprits, who have the right attitude, can be the architects of success.

3. To see life as a never-ending path of perfection, continuous improvement, and collaboration, because

small and big problems and small or big failures, are means for improvement and success.

This is a fundamental part of the Trustability culture.

When the light is made to be seen in areas of darkness, very prone to cause failures, an attitude of gratitude is achieved, which is the highest motivation there is. When you are grateful, it is because you are highly motivated and happy about something. It is in everyone's best interest to improve; no one likes mistakes or accidents, neither for himself nor for his family. Do not miss this opportunity in the companies, because it is what has the greatest impact on the culture of Trustability and its goals, which are wellbeing and the common good. It also motivates and integrates people.

If we analyze these 3 parameters and compare them with the following 3 parameters of culture, many times actual, real, we will see the road to change.

- **Person X**: hide problems so that no one notices, and you get out of trouble.
- **Person Y**: *it wasn't me; it was the other one.* I was *told to do so.*
- **Person Z**: criticizes again and again the bad, and the others, for their mistakes, magnifying them and, the more criticism, the more convincing, because they believe they have the solution.

There are many sectors that have this culture of untrustability. This culture of untrustability is often born in management. It is only by changing the culture at the management level that we can aspire to change it at the operational level, not before.

F14. MEASUREMENT AND DOCUMENTATION

There are at least 8 different types of documentation for companies and institutions, where everything must be written down so that there is evidence and history, both to evaluate the past and to reflect and improve the future. This is evidence of reliability in the management of the company.

1. Accounting and related financial documentation, including the legal aspect of minutes of meetings, board meetings, etc.
2. Process documentation, quality control and certification.
3. *ERP* software, which in addition to recording and documenting transactions, must also add observations and incidents.
4. Documentation of client relationships and transactions, e.g. *CRM*, evidencing agreements and observations, as well as transactions and satisfaction information.
5. Documentation of projects through all stages, from conception and initiation to completion and final results.
6. Documentation on organizational information, policies, procedures and regulations of the company and Human Resources files.
7. Documentation on Trustability Diagnostics, on analysis of failures and defects that adopt the perspective of evidencing failures and incidents, the analysis of their causes and the opportunity costs incurred, as well as the results not obtained, which could have been obtained, and their correction plans.

8. Documentation on Objectives and Plans, derived from strategic planning processes and their follow-up.

For the improvement of Trustability, it is very common, in the companies, that it is necessary to create or reinforce the Type: 2, 4, 7 and 8 of Documentation.

In Type 2, the culture that adopts *ISO* Certification or other specific certifications can contribute greatly.

In Type 4, the client focus of the Trustability culture forces the completion of sales management processes, with client satisfaction measurements and opportunities to improve satisfaction.

In Type 7, documentation is very important to instill a culture of competitiveness. One thing is the results obtained and another thing is the results that could be obtained if faults and defects were resolved.

This information is produced in improvement teams, quality circles, planning processes, interdisciplinary work teams, problem solving, and problem-oriented training.

NON-QUALITY costs are all those items, such as materials and labor, that cost and should not cost; they are superfluous and unnecessary if things were done right the first time. That is, according to a *stoichiometric* must be. This information belongs to type 7, documentation.

The *stoichiometric* is a formula used in engineering and science, especially in chemistry, to express that energy is not created, it is only transformed and, therefore, what goes in is what must come out.

It is about measuring what goes in, what is transformed, and then, what comes out under the perspective of measured energy (in calories or in some other form). The same amount of energy that goes in, is the energy that must come out, except if there is some energy that is lost, but that must be managed, accounted for, harnessed. Trustability means being responsible with what you handle, knowing and managing the energy you receive, handle, and deliver in the form of product or service.

Do you think a person is trustworthy when he wastes valuable energy and does not even know where it went? The answer is no, because sooner or later, life will charge you the bill for that mismanaged, wasted, squandered or stolen energy without conscience. Your time and the time of others, hours, is a very valuable and scarce resource and measure of energy use (maximum 100 years of life, say, if you are doing well and, to be available for certain matters, only maybe 8 hours or less a day). Being trustworthy to others and to yourself carries with it the great responsibility of managing your time and the time of others well.

In Type 1 documentation, there is only the perspective of results obtained, but there is an element that is the budget, which makes it necessary to compare the results obtained. In a highly competitive company, this budget should be prepared using information produced by Type 7 information management, based on the costs of NON-QUALITY. But it is not common, because the financiers, who make the budgets, do not handle this type 7 information specialty. Sometimes, the account catalogs of the accounting system are so generic that they only count as cost everything purchased of a given material, and do not distinguish between purchased and consumed, purchased, and not consumed. This is a cost breakdown of NON-QUALITY.

In Type 8, Documentation, each well thought-out objective must be accompanied by its goal and performance indicators, or *Key Performance Indicators* (KPIs).

An example of performance indicators, in objectives related to World 1, of the operation, can be found in what has already been mentioned in this book, in *Factor 10: Execution and Verification*, with the example of volume obtained in kilograms, first quality, second quality, direct cost per kilo, reworks per shift, etc.

In addition, in World 1, there is also client satisfaction as one of the key KPI's, i.e. Type 4 information.

In World 3, in the Finance function, there are many indicators of financial health, so that they must be observed month by month, and deviations must be pointed out and corrected, in the areas of working capital, debt, accounts receivable, gross profit, margin, profitability to sales, profitability to capital, among others.

In World 3, in the Human Capital function, turnover, training, absenteeism, overtime, accidents, are key indicators.

In World 2, the important thing is that the results of the whole are obtained; that the objectives with their corresponding indicators are met. This is the indicator for World 2. Were the objectives met? Were your team's results achieved? In what proportion? This percentage is a performance indicator for World 2, the World of Leaders. In addition to these indicators, we have the indicator of the health of the work environment and the company's image, which are a support for the company's sustainability, so that it can continue to obtain good results.

F15. CONTINUOUS IMPROVEMENT AND INNOVATION

F15.1. Innovation Processes

Generally, these are the steps that are followed in a Trustworthy innovation:

1. Identification of the need or area of opportunity.
2. Evaluation, if it is a need that, by solving and satisfying it, creates value.
3. Diagnosis of causes that originate this need. Understanding how the need arises.
4. Options for possible solutions to meet this need. First, describing what the solution consists of.
5. Evaluation of the different options, deciding, to what extent, to go deeper into each of them, in order to be able to appraise your investment and its value creation.
6. Specification of deliverables.
7. Decision making to select the winning option.
8. Refine the specifications of the deliverables of the selected option.
9. Work plan to develop the winning option, which generally consists of:
    9.1. Solution design engineering.
    9.2. Work plan with responsible parties, start and end dates for each activity.
    9.3. Costing of the work plan and estimation of the required investment.
    9.4. Quality control for testing.
    9.5. Follow-up and supervision.

9.6. Delivery based on specified agreements.

10. Marketing of the final product application:

   10.1. Market research.

   10.2. Product presentation.

   10.3. Introduction strategy.

   10.4. Implementation plan.

   10.5. Evaluation, follow-up, and control.

The link established in *Factor 13*: *Failure Detection and Learning from Mistakes,* which we analyzed earlier, is the beginning of a huge field of development for improvement and innovation.

Here we are going to deploy it to its full potential but recognizing that it connects to a new pole of development at its end: Research and Development, which is a major issue.

The paths that open up are as follows:

1. Continuous improvement, based on small details of correction and solution.
2. Process modification.
3. Process reengineering.
4. New product development.
5. Innovation projects.
6. Research and development (new *know-how*).
7. Research and development of *know why* and create knowledge.

F15.2. Continuous Improvement

Continuous improvement is required because change is continuous and permanent. These improvements can be made within the traditional organization structure, *boss-collaborators*, with unity of command, when a parameter of controlled flexibility in time, cost, order, and appropriate speed is introduced. Continuous and orderly improvement. To carry out this function, there is a wide range of possibilities. From continuous improvement meetings from time to time, quality circles with interdisciplinary teams, to high performance teams or parallel structures of analysis and problem solving, with people trained in it *(black belts* in analysis and problem solving).

We have to revolutionize leadership with the delegation I talked about in *Factor 3: Institutional Leadership*, in item 3.3: *Openness in Decision and Authority Perspectives*. Include and open up the perspective of each manager, using other sources of reference for decision making: Your next step in the production chain, your internal client, external client, and your technical support group.

In *Factor 19: Human Development Strategies*, I will address the topic of Socio-technical Leadership, which consists, precisely, in achieving a higher level in operational decision-making, with fewer bosses, more High Trustability operators, technically and humanely developed. Trustworthy People.

F15.3. Process Modification

People who already have an acquired view of failures in the current process are the most qualified to perform the so-called process modification to achieve higher Trustability.

Of course, it is necessary to consider the workshop blindness that some have more than others, so that, sometimes, some people do not perceive more efficient ways to change.

Other people, who may have a correct vision to be invited to the modification of processes, are the people who have witnessed the quality failures, in the function of Quality Control of products and protagonists in the evaluation.

There are specialists in process modification, which are also very important, especially in the most complex processes that require 3 technical elements:

1. Mastery of the technology involved and vision of the complete process.
2. Design, Redesign or Reengineering skills.
3. Skills to manage change processes, harmonizing disruption, for the benefit of the current client.

Finally, turning to machinery equipment suppliers can be helpful in modifying processes in some cases.

F15.4. Process Reengineering

Process Reengineering refers to first visualizing and then changing the so-called macro-processes of the entire company or institution, and then all the specific processes of each macro-process, reorienting them to serve the end client, the external client, in the most efficient way possible.

Online information and systems technology, digitalization and automation are of great importance in making all these processes more efficient through reengineering, including the programming and development of the appropriate software, to use all this strength to automate, streamline and improve client service, customizing their needs and their assortment, right to their home.

Personalization is the clearest trend to pursue in the coming years.

Who makes the most trustworthy reengineering?

Perhaps IBM, as advanced as it is in its *AI* process: Artificial Intelligence.

Sometimes, it is advisable to separate these 2 specialties: first, to reengineer the current information processes, then to automate, because it is impossible to do them well if they are tried to be done together.

TESLA: is the product of a reengineering of the automotive industry.

AMAZON: is the product of a reengineering of the commercial sector of consumer products.

GOOGLE: is a reengineering of location and route maps.

APPLE: is a reengineering of personalized remote communication.

SUPERMARKETS: they are a reengineering of the counter stores.

AMAZON SUPERMARKET: is a reengineering of self-service.

F15.5. New Product Development

There are some companies that aim to create new products and force themselves to obtain sales results, specifically talking about the new products created, developed, and implemented.

In these cases, there are specialized departments, staffed by people with research, development, creativity, and market introduction profiles.

The natural evolution of the life cycle of products and of the competition requires constant updating of products and their applications.

In today's world, change is constant, and the company that does not have the energy and discipline to develop new products and relevant modifications can easily be left out of the market.

To be trustworthy, in this function, means, first, to be competent in modifications and adaptations of the current product, as a first step in the journey of this function.

The second stage consists of redesigns or substitutions of the current product or service, providing benefits of fitness for use, customizing uses, or decreasing the cost when it is elastic to demand.

An example of new product development is what is currently happening with movies (formerly in movie theaters and now in homes), in education (formerly in classrooms and now online courses), and in many sectors such as automotive, aeronautics, space navigation, etc.

F15.6. Innovation Projects

The Japanese have been very successful in instilling and developing, in work teams, innovation in the perfection of products and also in processes. Their ability to focus on details and correct faulty details has made them very trustworthy, and with that, very successful.

Launching a cost reduction project and aligning all efforts to that Project/Objective, makes it possible to chain many innovation projects and result in a great overall result.

Other companies launch an innovation philosophy, a coordinator to select the best ideas and develop each one according to a resource budget.

Other companies have an innovation department, and undertake the development of new products, new processes, or new businesses on an ongoing basis.

In the case of New Businesses, this function must be combined with the Strategic Planning function, which specializes in Business Strategies and is very innovative.

F15.7. Research and Development

In the case of Research and Development areas, with high-tech laboratories, it is out of the focus of this book.

Trustability in Research and Development and how to mitigate risks in these investments is a very interesting area, which is only undertaken by large companies, large capitals, or universities. An example of this is the Bill and Melinda Gates Foundation, where they have channeled large sums of money to create new solutions to social problems of disease.

F16. CONTINUOUS COMMUNICATION OF RESULTS AND VALUES

In the *20 Factors* of the *Model to Build Trust HO*, we can observe that people are treated as adults, because they are made aware of the final product of their work, the final client, the internal client, the production chain, and their participation to eliminate failures, master their process, eliminate defects, and receive training.

This person, thus treated, thus educated, will have a greater scope in their contribution to the company. More productive and intelligent.

This is a value, the value of contributing more, the value of being treated as a responsible, important adult, as a partner, to a certain extent, and this is the cause of having a greater recognition of their worth and, therefore, of their self-esteem, motivation, and satisfaction. The individual becomes a crucial element in achieving certain goals that, if it were not for their worth, dedication and training, could not be achieved.

This feeling that results from an enriched, empowered job is one of the most important motivations in the lives of working people. Perhaps, the most important. This motivation is a cause of satisfaction and happiness when there are magnificent *scores* achieved, magnificent treatment of people and magnificent teamwork. Good Results, with Good Personal Contribution, with Good Treatment and Recognition received. The formula for sustainable trustability.

This means that the level of communication has already changed and, consequently, it is congruent with this new level, that this worker, collaborator, or partner, knows the general results of the company, and sees how the ship is going where everyone is going and that everyone must take care of.

It is required to communicate the overall results of the company to all participants. To be congruent with the quality in the treatment of people. *You belong to the ship's crew, and I tell you how the ship is doing.* That's the Trustworthy deal. It does not need to be a detailed communication in financial details or anything like that, it should be a communication designed for each audience. Leaders need to come across as trustworthy to their people.

In addition, there should be communication by area, on how the area is doing and, individually, how each one's performance has been. Of course, the best way to measure performance is to know your personal *score*, your interventions and the results of each intervention, your moves, your successes, your failures, the defects of the product you had to handle, your speed, etc.

The final *score* of the production chain should also be technically reported, especially if it is under the company's control. This is transparency throughout the chain. This improves performance and makes the entire production chain more trustworthy. Transparency of information, to improve the final *score*, is vital.

The only true and trustworthy thing to do is to recognize, in truth, that the results are due to everyone, to one extent or another.

Communicating Results is the tangible part of one side of the coin, and the other side is the intangible part that is discovered with the following questions that always come along with it:

Are they correct? Are these results trustworthy?

Who were the internal contributors to these results?

Thanks to whom, in terms of the external part of the company?

If there are profits, how will they be distributed? Is it possible to repeat them or are they one-time?

To answer these questions, it is necessary to have values. Values of honesty so that the information is true; of trustworthiness, so that the client trusts you; value of effort and dedicated work to be able to comply; value of causing benefits to clients; value of teamwork; value of common wellbeing.

Results and Values go together.

Results need to be Trustworthy, they need to be true, whether they are good or bad. If they are bad and they communicate and publish them as good, they are unfairly seeking undeserved gratification. If they are good and publish them as bad, they are unfairly seeking to avoid a payment that is legal or fair. In both cases, a lack of Trustability is committed.

Results and Values go hand in hand, and the impact on the company's Trustability culture is very large.

It is recommended to work with values and to exemplify those values in each position, in each area or trade, since the indispensable lubricant for there to be Results are the Values. If there is no lubricant, the machine will not produce results, it will break down.

F17. PRACTICAL POLICIES, LAWS AND REGULATIONS

Laws and regulations that are very objective and practical are required to achieve order and consistent unity of command. Communicate them and train people in them. Laws and regulations must strike a balance between leaving people free, motivating them to do and controlling their actions, between the rights they grant and the obligations they demand, in order to be congruent with the formula of Giving and Receiving mentioned in *Factor 6: Care for Customer and User*, of this section.

It is very common the lack of emotional maturity to make this balance and the lack of intelligent dialogue between the parties, lack of convening power of the leader and specialized leaders in a better design of laws and regulations that privilege the current and future quality of life.

The policies that should be clear and established, at least, should be the following:

- Corporate Governance, Meetings, Board, and other legal considerations, in accordance with the company's Articles of Incorporation.
- Investments and Investment Projects. Decision authority.
- Dealing with clients, including sales, credit, commissions, and other relevant matters.
- Internal and external audit.
- Of legal obligations in serious cases with clients and the community.
- Insurance and risk management. Occupational accidents.
- Fiscal and administrative accounting.
- Changes in organizational structures and positions.
- Selection of collaborating personnel.
- Hiring of collaborating personnel.
- Internal work regulations and discipline.
- Remuneration and benefits to collaborating personnel.
- Collective bargaining agreements.
- Training and development.

- Administration of labor laws and regulations.
- Provider relations.
- Management of Conflicts of Interest.
- Privacy in the handling of personal data.
- Technological secrecy.
- Internal communication and corporate image.
- Public Relations and travel expenses.
- Regulation of office and *home office* spaces.

F18. AUDIT

An auditing system is required to provide an internal control to resolve the resulting natural Conflicts of Interest, to monitor and correct things out of order, on an ongoing basis, with a professionally performed auditing approach.

Human nature has a very strong part, where the person is naturally and automatically driven by the most comfortable path, the one that is the easiest, the one with the least effort, the one that gives you the most immediate benefit. The body does the same, it seeks to accommodate itself to rest, to economy of movement, to not being in a hurry, to not doing. This part of human nature tends to fulfill very well the function of receiving, of obtaining in order to live, which is needed.

On the other hand, the experiences of life, survival, self-improvement, the need for security and to avoid illness, to avoid conflicts with other people, brings out the other human nature, that of we cannot live if we do not move, with effort and sometimes sacrifice, to solve human needs, first the essential ones, and then the additional ones.

It is discovered humanly that it is necessary to counteract that part of human nature, prepared to receive, with the other part of human nature, in which it is necessary to give, to move, to pay, to work, in order to be able to live.

We also discover that in order to live we need others. It is discovered that if one human does one thing, and another human does a complementary thing, and they share them, the goal of living is more easily achieved.

One discovers that it is necessary to give in order to receive. This second part of human nature is as indispensable and essential as the first.

This balance of the 2 human natures (Receiving and Giving) must be well channeled. The first part, that of receiving, is automatic, without thinking and letting yourself go; the second part, that of giving, must be done by thinking and redirecting the body's actions, to do something worthwhile, that makes sense, that produces well-being, even if it costs effort and even sacrifice.

The reward obtained from going for the second part of human nature (giving), is greater and more satisfying, but it is not immediate, it comes after trying several times, until it gives results. It costs.

Immediate solution vs. worked solution. In the second human nature (giving), there is a lot of reasoning to understand and redirect, but also the heart to feel that the effort makes sense. Reason and feeling; thoughts and emotions.

Reasoning (strengths of mind) helps for the following processes:

- Thinking to analyze.

- Thinking to decide.
- Thinking to plan or visioning.
- Thinking to judge.
- Thinking to do (execute, remediate, correct, improvise, undertake).
- Thinking to reason out feelings and emotions.

The Audit function is mainly involved in Thinking for Judging. However, the next link in the chain is Thinking to Correct; that is, within Thinking to Do, it goes to Thinking to Correct.

However, in order to be able to correct beforehand, it is necessary to define a *"should be "* in order to compare it with what actually happens and identify the deviation or failure.

We have already dedicated an entire section to failure analysis and lessons learned. The *Audit* function is an extension of *Factor 13*: *Failure Detection and Learning from Mistakes*, applied to administrative processes.

This is where Ethics and Morals come in, to identify this *duty to be*.

Yes, there is a tendency in human nature to *take advantage*. The easiest way to make a profit at the expense of others. When an unethical, non-moral action is allowed, this action of the person leads to a destructive process against himself and against others. This criminal, conflictive behavior must be formally avoided in organizations. The audit serves this fundamental purpose.

It is good for the human person to feel watched, because their behavior is improved; it is improved by making them think about avoiding natural tendencies that will subtract them from harm, in order to achieve a greater well-being.

It must make sense why the surveillance. The person feels a loss of freedom, there is a natural tendency to reject surveillance.

The thesis of this book is to explain and grasp the meaning of well-founded and well-exercised auditing, in order to achieve good results of trustworthy wellbeing.

Explained in this way, it is necessary to have an audit function that is transparent and explained throughout the organization.

Unfortunately, traditional auditing is understood as an accounting matter, the auditing of accounts, and that vision is very narrow, and if it is not expanded to what I am exposing here, the understanding of the function and its acceptance is deficient, by its internal clients and by its users. This is very serious.

A serious sin of the audit function is to focus on unimportant events without well-analyzed causalities. If it is not capable of producing felt benefits, it is a bureaucratic audit, with emotional complexes of its author.

An auditor must have a profile of being motivated and capable for substantial improvement. Materiality in the Recommendations.

A Trustworthy Audit function is one that serves the following:

- Prevent money leaks out of the company's order.
- Check the reliability of accounting information and financial information (quality control of financial information).
- Check the Trustability of the information fed to Accounting.

- Monitor and drive the organization to respect and obey well-defined policies, verifying adherence to the policy or regulation.
- Help design company policies, but not as judge and jury, but as an impartial advisor.
- Audit of certifications, which is usually performed by experts from the certifying entity.
- Audits to protect the security and reliability of digital and Internet systems.

There are 6 types of audits:

1. The Audit of Accounts, to have accounting Trustability and to avoid asset leaks.
2. The Audit of Management Policies.
3. The Operational Audit to deepen in processes that have internal control weaknesses and are to avoid possible money leaks or false information.
4. Information Technology Audit, to protect the security of computer systems and the Internet.
5. Audit of Conflicts of Interest, in legal and institutional matters, avoiding serious cases and fraud.
6. The audit to ensure that the certification granted is still in force and valid.

The Audit Function mainly benefits:

- Shareholders of the company.
- Clients.
- Workers and collaborators.

- Third parties, such as government, suppliers, and community.

F19. HUMAN DEVELOPMENT STRATEGIES

F19.1. Trustability Achievement Recognition

It is necessary to objectively recognize true successes and trustworthy people, making them participate more and with greater responsibility, merit, and compensation, so that they lead the most demanding and difficult tasks. In a given problem and its solution, in a given project or task, the Trusted person is more valuable and contributory, so why not distinguish and motivate them?

There is a bad practice and culture: hiding the merits of some employees, on the part of self-conscious bosses, which does a lot of harm. The object is that those who have no merit feel at ease not to be compared and not to be traumatized. Mainly, the boss who feels that he or she could be displaced by one of the very trustworthy people. This communist and Machiavellian inspired practice has been abused; it discourages those who have merit, incurring in a culture of mediocrity and encouraging incapacities, comfort, and *status quo*; of course, resulting in promoting a society without correct and trustworthy solutions to problems, nor substantial progress.

The opportunity cost incurred by this is enormous. What is left undone by a culture of mediocrity and bureaucracy, the opportunities that are left unattended and not even seen, or by following directions that do not lead to real solutions that cause more problems, when trustworthy talent is left untapped, and unreliable bosses are put in important positions.

Another very wrong practice is not to promote the search for improvement opportunities, the identification of problems and the competition to solve them.

Another mistaken practice is what is said: the one who advances is frowned upon by his peers and they are dedicated to knock him down. There are environments where it is normal practice.

Another very wrong practice is not to promote those who have reliable achievements, because there is no more room, since all the positions are occupied; in other words, the one who reaches a position, despite doing harm, has preference over the one who can improve everyone?

When it comes, specifically, to finding solutions, especially to difficult problems, is when you have to go to the most capable and trustworthy people. In the last twenty years, there has been a great demotivation of young people to be experts, to be Highly Trustworthy, hard-working, specialized, useful to others by being champions.

A possible cause of this demotivation is an education received, that *we only have one life and that we have to enjoy it*, second by second, in something of personal taste, not to go around serving others or being subordinate. To be CEO of one's own life, based on little experience, high tastes, and desires. Poor and wrong education, because it is hiding from them the richest part of life, the one that begins or contains some things that do not like at first, but if you master them, you end up appreciating them and becoming passionate about them, because of the great impact they have on you by overcoming you.

The quality of being expert and trustworthy is not shown with arrogance or reckless presumptions, it is shown with facts in practice and with good humble spirit, of helping others to climb steps in the perfection of something worthwhile. When arrogance is shown, it diminishes objectivity, simplicity, and negatively affects Trustability.

The one who gives the most opinion should be the most competent and trustworthy in the subject at issue, not the one who is the most popular or the most political.

There is a method that weights, according to the person's history of success and reliability, the weight of different people's opinions in a consensus. This is more democratic, fair, and convenient for all, than equality of weight in opinions. In a committee of doctors studying a solution, this distinction and weighting is naturally made.

In medicine, in aviation, in international sports, in science and in industry, Trustability is valued, and Trustworthy people are recognized, allowing, and promoting the most Trustworthy people to stand out and light the way for others. All the positions in the sectors that are open to the search for the highest Trustability are never filled.

Highly Trustworthy people receive their most desired reward when they are consulted, they are listened to, and there are better results with their intervention. Better results are a bigger prize than a medal at a dinner or party.

Trustworthy people know that everything costs, that getting to where they have cost, and that postponing gratification is worth it.

Specialties and trades are jealous, so that if you stop doing them, you lose skill and ability in executing them. You have obligations and demands to keep you at a high level, it's not for free.

Trustability in what is being done now is just as important as Trustability in thinking about what needs to be changed, what new things could be done to improve the result, so that the usefulness to others increases. That is what the *Model to Build Trust HO* is all about. Both talents must be recognized.

It is not true that the Trustworthy are only interested in medals, (this may be a Machiavellian criticism) see them, observe them and you will see that what they are interested in is the action in their trade, specialty or profession, the facts, the execution, to act again and not waste time receiving medals, which are good, but up to a certain point. The best satisfaction is obtained in the exercise, in the execution, in the game itself, not on the table, off the court.

The space that exists to do better the things that are done is very large, and if you find a very trustworthy person and, moreover, with the potential to create value, making the product, the service, or the human relationship more valuable, there will always be an opportunity to promote it adequately. Of course, not too fast, so as not to obtain results, and not too slow, so as to spoil, but if it gives more, it is always possible to promote it further.

F19.2. Participatory Socio-Technical Leadership

Delegate using biunivocal correspondence: Delegated responsibility, on the one hand, and Competencies, with good, demonstrated, and proven attitudes, on the other hand. Empower based on Responsibility, Competence, and attitude, shown, and validated.

F19.3. The Right Person in the Right Position

To enrich the position within certain limits, increasing responsibility along with increasing demonstrated competencies. Playing this wonderful method of having more responsibility, as you demonstrate more skills, more achievements for the good of the trade, product, process, client, and the company. Increasingly participative administration in technical improvement decisions. The technology to produce and deliver the product has areas of opportunity that can be addressed dynamically, delegating, according to the progress of the position's mastery. There is almost no limit. There is always something additional, positive, that creates value.

When the person is also an informal leader of colleagues, the circle is closed to empower, enrich the position, and promote the person. This is when the person becomes rounded because they are technically and socially skilled. They are very valuable people, both for solving technical problems and gaining technical Trustability, as well as for coordinating their colleagues on the basis of personal and human dignity.

F19.4. Continuous Training in the Trade

Training is required, both Self-taught, as well as Formal and Practical *Coaching* on the fly, in technical aspects of the trade. Identify the levels of Beginner, Intermediate, Advanced and Expert or Master, in each trade or specialty. Establish a Training Policy, depending on the technical competence of the position and the people's mastery of the position. Spend at least two weeks a year on training with paid company time. These two weeks can be spent on the technical stuff, on the

Model to Build Trust HO, or on Emotional Intelligence. First, starting with the necessary training for job mastery; then, in the *Model to Build Trust*; then, in Emotional Intelligence; finally, in positions that are part of their career in the company.

Training must be self-sustaining. To be able to demonstrate that what the training added, in the practice of the work, was useful and productive.

Apply the concept of the Provider-Client-User chain, to demonstrate that the training is from a Trustworthy provider, which measures the positive results and satisfaction of its internal clients and users. Training that is applied on the job, that is followed up and that corresponds to work systems adopted by the company. It is highly recommended to use, when possible, internal experts in some specialty to provide training to new employees.

F19.5. Continuous Training on the *Model to Build Trust HO.*

The Model to Build Trust HO, shown in this Chapter; the derivations of workshops, exercises, and consultancies on Trustability, which will be developed; the material, very rich that already exists in the market... there is a lot of literature, a path of continuous improvement can be formed, almost without limits, in the development of Trustability.

Quality tools such as *Pareto's Law* and the statistical bases of Quality Control must be taught to everyone. Stratification, classification, Gaussian Bell, Gant Diagram, Ishikawa Fishbone Diagram, failure analysis, operational planning, zero accidents, zero defects and other management processes for Trustworthy decision making should be taught with the guidance of the *Model to Build Trust HO.*

F19.6. Emotional Intelligence Training

Emotional Intelligence opens the fields already mentioned:

EMOTIONAL INTELLIGENCE FIELDS	PARAMETERS
EMOTIONAL STABILITY IN THE FACE OF ADVERSITY	Pressure Tolerance and Impulse Control
INTERPERSONAL SKILLS	Empathy, Assertiveness and Human Relationships
INSPIRATION TO OTHERS	Objectivity, Self-Realization with Emotional Stability, Assertiveness and Empathy
HAPPINESS AND FULFILLMENT	*True Self* Concept, Emotional Awareness and Happiness

Each person has a different advancement in their EQ profile.

First, you must know that profile and for this, there is a tool called *hsei*, which is explained in the book: *How to Be More Productive and Happier,* authored by me. Start by measuring the 16 Attributes of Emotional Intelligence to make a good diagnosis and embark on the journey of empowerment and self-improvement.

Then, depending on what is to be achieved, the development path is undertaken, based on the guidelines offered in the aforementioned book.

Self-taught, as well as Formal and Practical *Coaching* training is required on the go, in the strengthening of Emotional Intelligence.

A solid basis for developing Emotional Intelligence is not to personalize the human reactions of others. When dealing with issues, do not take as a personal attack the effects of individual human endeavors in combination with the endeavors of others.

Understand that there are natural Conflicts of Interest. There are frictions and there are human interactions, both rough and thorny, trivial, and innocuous as well as pleasant and favorable. These positive and negative reactions are caused by third parties, but reacting to an issue without knowing the whole, but only a small part of the reality. It is natural that your reaction is partial and incomplete. You don't have to take their reactions with your perspective, but you have to understand their perspective, which is often very incomplete. Therefore, you have to give yourself permission to be very tolerant. In the *True Self* there are no culprits, but only causes that cause effects, sometimes wrong, sometimes right, that impact on the person as a resource, only, so that those attacks or those praises are not of essence, but accidental. Both favorable and hostile effects are so ephemeral and superficial that it is necessary to detach oneself from personalizing, which only causes human conflicts and unproductivity. *If garbage is thrown at you, don't eat it,* throw it away.

F20. HUMAN MOTIVATION STRATEGIES

F20.1. Promotion of Values and their Application in Each Position

In *Factor 16: Continuous Communication of Results and Values*, it was commented how important it is to accompany the numbers and words that speak of financial results with values that support the obtaining, management and destination of the financial results achieved. They should give confidence in the Management submitting them.

Are they right, are they not too much, not too little, and what is going to be done with them, where are the benefits and how are they applied, what are the values that were used to achieve these results?

They are not for free, are they?

Honesty, service, technology, dedicated work, specialization, teamwork, Trustability (being trustworthy to others), empathy, good treatment, good image, being fair, being institutional, being formal, with social vision, cheerful and familiar, are examples of values that are generally needed to work and obtain lawful results that are a source of pride and satisfaction.

The trustworthy thing is not to mention them, but to practice them, and for that, it is necessary to put them in the words of each collaborator, which are translated into everyday actions, words that imply actions in the daily life inside and outside the workplace.

Values are internal: you either have them or you don't. If they are present, they are translated into actions and attitudes. They are not words; they are attitudes and actions.

In this case, it is necessary to choose some values that should be practiced together in order to reap good results as a whole.

Values help to tell you how good results were achieved, how you have to work to get good results, because they are not just any results that make you money; that is not getting money anyhow. Values also help you to know how to distribute the benefit of those results.

These values must be brought to life in each position, in each person, in each department of the organization.

First, a set of values is made; then, a consensus is reached among the people, until a description of values that makes sense to those who participated in this exercise is reached. The more participants, the better.

Then, write sentences representative of those values; afterwards, follow up to practice and recognize them. It is good that the people who best represent them in an experiential way are recognized, and that a public recognition is made to see them in the flesh. Make clear the value and merit for internalizing the value.

Creation of a Human, Social, Positive and Inclusive Environment of Respect and Collaboration.

In many countries, there is a genetic ingredient of very warm social human relations, which is widely evidenced when dealing with visitors with that human warmth of friendship, of social festivities of coexistence of all ages.

This beautiful human interaction has to be promoted within the limits of Trustability. Helping others, healthy socializing, talking, singing, and dancing, when there is no excess of alcohol, is generally very motivating and warm.

Also, when it comes to promoting sports, it is important to take care of impulse control to avoid fights in the game, it is convenient to anticipate with good rules. With these controls, social coexistence is very rich.

Often, it is better to offer sporting and family events than to pay them the equivalent cost in salary, since, with that salary, they would not be able to have these benefits. The ideal, as some large companies have done, is to own or partner with a family recreation center. According to the company's possibilities, the size can be modest, but very convenient.

In the case of governments, the citizen and neighborhood recreation parks are important because they always teach this magnificent culture of healthy social coexistence, where human relations flow with education, civility, and fun, coexisting among people of different ages. When talking about inclusive, it has been forgotten that the coexistence between different ages and generations is very important. Children living with adults teach these natural life cycles, in such a way that children become aware of what the different types of adults are like, identify themselves and can talk freely and confidently with them.

F20.2.   Physical and Emotional Health Promotion and Care

In some developed countries, there are standards that talk about taking care of people's physical integrity, health and emotional wear and tear.

The chapters to which it refers contain points that are very worthy of attention. Being trustworthy is a characteristic that helps a lot to exercise these rules correctly.

They mainly talk about the following:

- In case of traumatic accidents, provide psychological help.

- In case of emotional exhaustion, attend to them in order to avoid greater consequences.

- Organize functions and tasks well, to avoid unhealthy uncertainty.

- To have a favorable working environment for people.
- Survey people, to see their dissatisfactions and correct them as a whole.
- Avoidance of occupational accidents.
- Avoid sexual, labor and any other kind of harassment. If it happens, investigate it and sanction it according to the law.
- Avoid aggression, use of drugs and narcotics.

F20.3. Development of Work Purposes

You as a resource, to give a service to others, known in the back of your mind and heart, that you play a role of service to others, in exchange for something for you and your family. Giving and Receiving. In the short and long term.

What is the purpose of your work?

What do you get in this work game?

Sacrifice to serve more. It is good, but it has its limits and its correct administration, to avoid extremes or harmful excesses.

Being someone else's client, fine, but in exchange for what?

In *Chapter III*, we made it very clear that the purpose of Trustability is to benefit the wellbeing of you, your family, and the people with whom you live; finally your city, your state, your country.

Following this *Model to Build Trust HO* must first mesh with one's own well-being in terms of health, personal strengths, energy, and motivation to live. You can't give what you don't have. If you have well-being, you can give, both to yourself and to others. If you don't have wellness, if you are sick, you are too limited to give.

After your well-being, usually, follows the well-being of your family, partner, parents, children, and your children's education.

Family integration and work-family balance, in its different ways, is a key function of the *Model to Build Trust HO.* Close the cycle, close the clamp.

The other important goal is to prepare you for a dignified old age, rich in health, rich in being able to be self-sufficient and leave a good mark on this world.

It promotes savings together with austerity, that is, rational spending, with cost-benefit and opportunity cost criteria.

It is not true that money is to be spent, money is to be capitalized, living healthy and dignified lives with well-being. Spend what you need, save enough, and invest what you can to reap in the near future, which is known as postponing gratification, characteristic of Trustworthy and successful people.

It is said that the happiest age is from 60 to 70 years old, normally; of course, happier for those who can continue sowing, having fun and, at the same time, reaping what they have sown, saved, and invested during their active working life. This is wellbeing and capitalization.

It's like that Patek Philipe watch, advertised as a purchase not for you, but for your heirs, but you enjoy it. This is your patrimony, you enjoy it and what is left over, you inherit, but after using it. For that, it has to be built with work.

It works to live better, familiarly, and socially.

God, Family, Work, Savings, Recreation, Friends, Trustability, Well-being. No more is needed. The rest is superfluous, it is decapitalizing. Choose what is truly important and essential. If you confuse what is merely accidental, superfluous, with what is essential, you get into an insatiable pseudo-satisfier, which takes away well-being instead of giving it to you.

Plan for your old age to be very dignified, fun, and sufficiently strengthened.

It is also recommended to recognize seniority in the company and encourage socialization with senior colleagues in the company.

F20.4. Equity and Transcendence Environment

Several civilizations, such as the Indian, Jewish, Spanish, and Mexican, coincide with indigenous cultures, in thinking that death brings us more life, certainly, related in some way and consistent with what you have lived here on earth.

Some speak of reincarnation, which is more life, and others of spiritual life.

Those who think this way, intend to capitalize on this life, in order to achieve something good or more satisfactory in the afterlife.

The most common way is to pretend to connect, to help, in some way, the people you love.

The main consequence of this way of thinking, of continuity of life after death, is to pretend that there is a communication, a connection with known beings and loved ones in this life.

It provides our spiritual and social sides with a very powerful motivational stimulus.

To be able to continue more mature and fulfilling human relationships with our fellow human beings.

Recognizing people's seniority in the company and acknowledging beloved ancestors is something that gives very human motivation and hope.

Having one event a year where this type of supreme and true equality is recognized is motivating for everyone.

We are all going to die, just as our ancestors died and our children who are now living. In Japan, there is a very strong appreciation for senior citizens, because they are prepared for it from an early age. I am sure that, in Latin American countries, a culture of planning for old age and taking care of the elderly could be very well accepted, because in order to be revered as an old man, you need to demonstrate during your life, to be a good person to those around you. So, the long-term vision is very useful in the short term, it enriches your decisions on how to behave every day, by having that vision and that intention. That's a better education than a theoretical school class. A culture of preparing for old age, aiming for a healthy old age, would do a lot of good.

Finally, it is very convenient to carry out some acts of philanthropy with the community, on behalf of the company, inviting its workers and collaborators, summoning, promoting freely, and having rich experiences in results, sharing support resources, never forcing, never imposing, and that, provides the company with a Moral Authority.

II.3. MANAGEMENT OF THE MODEL TO BUILD TRUST HO.

There should be a person responsible for the maintenance of the Model, along with surveying users about their satisfaction. This results in adjustments and their evolution. Avoid the entropy to which everything accommodates. The person in charge must report their findings and take corrections and possible solutions congruent with those findings.

Being trustworthy in countries or places with high levels of corruption is not easy to achieve, but it is necessary for subsistence as societies.

These *Sections* of the *Model to Build Trust HO*, with *20 Factors* from *Section II.2*, to be implemented at the country level, can be achieved within two to three years if promoted extensively. At the same time, surprising Productivity, Quality, Personal Satisfaction and Union Results are obtained.

The Human Motivation factor, with a high social ingredient, is an important need for all people. It is proven that people who live longer are because they have a high connection and for them it is of high significance to have a close human relationship.

It is a lever to lay the foundations of Trustability, to procure the wellbeing of your loved ones by being Trustworthy, thus gaining their trust.

Trustability for friendship and companionship, is to offer help that is useful to others. Authentic attention. To meet a need.

This *Model to Build Trust HO*, accompanied by the workshops and courses provided by the *People Management Institute*, for the business world, for the world of schools and universities, for children, young people and finally, for experts in Trustability, can achieve the increase in Trustability that will make a country acquire credibility, sustained progress, and greater happiness, based on the pride of feeling: To be Useful, Productive, Trustworthy, Friendly, and Citizen Friendly.

II.4. CONFLICTS OF INTEREST

The way to correctly counteract, in a society, these natural human mechanisms to favor oneself over others is called: CONTROL OF CONFLICTS OF INTEREST.

It is a human mechanism, but also a social one, to assert the truth and the perspective that our neighbor is an extension of ourselves.

In order to achieve Trustability, it is necessary to free ourselves from Conflicts of Interest.

In order to achieve Trustability it is necessary to decide to solve the Conflict of Interest which, in the political case, is about being congruent between continuing to have power at all costs and achieving the truth and the common good at all costs.

You can't have both at the same time in many issues and situations.

There are several reasons for this conflict of interest:

1. Confusion between *what should be done by law, well done, and agreed upon,* and what should be *done by the will of the leader*. The greater the lack of laws, approved and consensual customs, the more room there is for the application of the leader's will.

2. The more space the application of the leader's will occupies, by human nature, the more the leader will do what preserves their power, even if it is not the best solution for everyone.

3. Confusion between what is appropriate to act by science and experts, especially in some very

advanced matters, against the will of the leader, who is not an expert in the matter they are deciding.

4. Low culture and education are ingredients of non-reliability and non-congruence.

In the Constitution of the United States, it is said that power comes from all citizens, equal, because they are children of God, and that when a leader or president is appointed, this higher power must be preserved in the citizens and not in the ruler. The rights of citizens are connatural to individuals, and the citizens decide to organize themselves for public administration, very well delimiting the government.

Citizens should not expect the government to solve everything for them, but on the contrary, it is often worse and more expensive to depend on the government, because when the government intervenes, it becomes politicized, bureaucratized, and local sensitivity is lost, and the government's solution is more expensive. This develops in the citizens an attitude that it is better to do it ourselves, and only turn to the government for essential public administration matters. That makes for better and more capable citizens and, therefore, a better country. This makes citizens concerned about resolving their issues, without help, collaborating and contributing, so as not to depend on the government.

It is more trustworthy to solve the problems directly and not to depend on the center, which is far from the problem, when they do not even know it well. This increases efficiency and trustability.

If it is in human nature to try to preserve and increase the power of the leader, then the only right thing to do is to limit the authority and power of the ruler, as the U.S. *Constitution* does, and that increases the reliability of the country. If left to the will of the ruler, it will produce results contrary to Trustability.

- What happens, socially, when there is Conflict, between the heartfelt truth and the customs of lack of objectivity?
    - *The group puts pressure to preserve the customs. It is very likely that habit will win out over evidence of objectivity. Often the status quo is preferred to the heartfelt truth.*
- What happens, socially, when there is Conflict, between the heartfelt truth and the leader's will?
    - *Generally, the leader surrounds them with people loyal to them, and those people only communicate what the leader wants to hear. So, people's heartfelt truth is not considered.*

A very serious side effect, which spreads like cancer, is that the good, the successful, the achievers, those who have merit for their contribution to development and progress, those who have made capital for themselves, are criticized, and sometimes demonized by cultures of low trustworthiness.

There are only two options: either you seek consensus for a common good, which does not give you strength power, but only moral power, or you go down other possible paths, to defeat, through force, the others.

The consequences are very different depending on which path society has chosen.

Obviously, in many countries, only the option of fighting opposing sides with war and strength is valid.

Obviously, in the past, the acquisition of central power was done through wars, and the one who triumphed in the war, kept the power.

Later, it turned into factional wars, but wars and deaths, after all, albeit more selective.

In countries where a consensus-based policy can be implemented, there must be at least 3 operating rules:

1. A central government without major privileges.

2. Rules of competence, quality, and peace, to appoint the president, where reason, competence and peace are guaranteed.

3. A government bounded by society and by its limited intervention of power.

And it should not be forgotten that, in several indigenous peoples, there is central power, without internal wars, as in the case of the Tarahumara (Rarámuris) in Mexico, who meet the 3 operating rules mentioned in the previous paragraph. Of course, in that culture, there is not much to be had of superior privileges since everyone lives very austerely. I do not mean that this characteristic of passivity, in the growth of satisfiers, is a basic and required condition in the High Model to Build Trust I am proposing. They are two different cultures, and in both cultures, it is possible to be High Trustability, respecting their philosophy of life.

The main conflicts of interest that arise are in the following areas:

- Money and money agreements, between partners and within the legal framework.

- Money and money agreements, between company and employees, between bosses and collaborators, with colleagues, clients, suppliers, third parties.
- Appointment decisions in positions or granting of powers of attorney of the company.
- Accounting or management information, Trustworthy or Unreliable.
- Human Relations with impartiality or lack of impartiality of judgment.
- Secrecy in matters of technology, human relations, sensitive information, reserved information, disabilities and illnesses, confidential information, and private information.
- Role confusion between being directly responsible or being indirectly responsible or not being responsible.

The main causes of Conflicts of Interest are the following:

- Personal economic benefit or detriment.
- Family economic benefit or detriment.
- Benefit or detriment to fame or good personal image.
- Benefits or detriments to fame or family image.
- Benefit or detriment of favoring oneself by discovering confidential and sensitive information.
- Benefiting from human attachments and preferences, whether for reasons of sex, familiarity, fraternity, hatred, conflicting backgrounds, interests contrary to the company and to the dignity of people, which infringe on the decision-making capacity of a manager, who must look after the interests of the company and the policies and laws in force.

Solutions for a better control and mitigation of Conflicts of Interest, that is, to avoid own responsibilities, poorly done, blaming others, and avoid any vulnerability for affective or family, sexual, or fraternal reasons, are the following:

1. Correct structure of well-organized roles.
2. Code of Ethics in force and Conflict of Interest Control policies and regulations.
3. Audit and internal control.
4. External auditor.
5. Reports and complaints mailbox, handled with excellent confidentiality and efficiency.
6. Exhaustive investigation in cases of loss or embezzlement.
7. Exemplary leadership that creates a good work environment, with formal and informal leaders, conditioned and trained in Trustability.
8. High-tech observation mechanisms.
9. Positive reinforcements to reward Trustability and reinforcing sanctions to punish lack of Trustability.
10. Values formation, with specific translation in each specialty area.

II.5. COMPLEMENTARY EXPLANATIONS TO THE MODEL

1. WHY SHOULD WE BE TRUSTWORTHY?

In matters of high difficulty and complexity, the correct method is not the egalitarian popular democracy of the universal vote, but human nature discovers who is the person who should help and collaborate the most, depending on the issue at hand.

If in a highly complex technical matter, they try to solve it with friends who do not master the subject, but are faithful; or with people who handle dogmas of social and philosophical ideology, who do not solve the subject, but manipulate with theories and politics; or with technicians who do not manage to translate their technical solutions to understandable terrain for their clients and their users, who are theoretical technicians: well, the three approaches, the three cases mentioned, are NOT TRUSTWORTHY.

It is not about cronyism, it is not about general political ideology, which subordinates everything to its type of thinking, but it is about an appropriate contribution according to the subject, according to the type of problem, taking advantage of the best of each one. Therefore, differences in knowledge, aptitude, attitude, and vocation among individuals set the tone for specialization. In this sense, these differences mark the natural selection, so that each one contributes to the extent of its possibilities to benefit the whole.

The whole requires many issues to move forward and build a better life, just like each person, because we are faced with the following: to be born, to be cured of diseases, to be saved from accidents and unwanted attacks; to eat, drink, sleep, rest, socialize, do sports and entertainment, culture and art; to be educated, get married, transport, create new knowledge, create solutions for life, have satisfactions, reproduce, grow and transcend.

Wisdom, freedom, positive creativity and serving others is the only way to face and overcome these challenges.

This requires a democracy centered on Values, on recognized merits of positive influence on others, and the way to achieve this is for citizens to be Trustworthy in what we specialize in, in our lives and in our interaction with others.

Real life should be lightened by the people who are the most Trustworthy and not by resentful activists against society, focused on their victim case. Society pays a very high price of self-destruction when the leader tries to make light of being a victim. The Trusted Ones do not focus on their own case, they focus on a solution for all and for the whole to live better.

In real life everyone feels what is progress or regression, it is something perceived and heartfelt. The Most Trustworthy have the responsibility to seek long-term improvement as well as short-term improvement that motivates.

The most trustworthy is irremediably condemned to succeed in their mission, sooner or later, because they stick to exactly what they offer.

The untrustworthy person bets that, by chance or by having a *supposedly* good intention, success will happen they are irremediably condemned to fail.

At the end of the road, between the Trustworthy and the Untrustworthy, the following happens: *To the one who has more, more will be given, and to the one who has less, the little will be taken away.*

The Trustworthy people will produce sustainable benefits to others because they enter the world of abundance, while the Untrustworthy will produce resentment and enter the world of scarcity, for themselves and for those around them.

2. CONSEQUENCES OF BEING TRUSTWORTHY

- In case of doubts from others, they turn to the Trusted Person.
- They do not betray.
- Do not decide without foundation and experience.
- They are not afraid of the truth.
- They do not lie on purpose.
- They apologize when they realize they made a mistake and regret the negative consequences, regardless, temporarily lose face, and help to correct the mistake.
- They do not have a double agenda, but only one side.
- Be wary of people who cheat.
- They have an aversion to deception and lying.
- Speak and act on what you do know and are sure of.
- They prefer to say I don't know, when they do not know, than to improvise with witticisms and reckless bets.
- You are aware of what is certain, what can be, what cannot be and the impact on others.

- They hit and score many times more often than they miss.
- They project charisma in what they do know.
- In an environment where merit is what counts, the Trustworthy person is selected over the not-so-Trustworthy.

3. CONSEQUENCES OF NOT BEING TRUSTWORTHY

- People who know this person do not believe in them.
- It is necessary to verify their assessments and assertions elsewhere.
- They distrust everyone because they know they are untrustworthy and project themselves as untrustworthy to others.
- Betray.
- Distrust the truth. Run away from the truth.
- They consider themselves to be magicians of deception, and they claim to be smarter than others, whom they deceive.
- They speak and act in many ways (multi-roles) projecting to sell their charismatic image, to counteract their lack of competence.
- They prefer to improvise and be superficial.
- In their achievements, they do not have as many successes as they say they have.
- Shun the Trustworthy.
- They have a double agenda. Two-faced.

- They have an aversion for *the detail of detail*.
- Promote Untrustworthiness by their example and actions.
- It spreads corruption, giving short-term benefits to many more.
- It is easy for them to choose to steal.
- It is easy for them to choose to buy with money, that which, under reliable circumstances, it is not lawful to buy.

We have in the world and in human nature, a struggle between the Culture with tendencies of low or No Trustability, which is corruption, idleness and *gandalla culture*, against the Culture of high or medium Trustability. In some fields, one wins more than the other.

He who does not compromise does not advance it is a colloquial phrase widely used in some cultures. It represents the culture of corruption and unreliability.

Thief who robs a thief has a hundred years of forgiveness: this is another phrase that represents the culture of untrustworthiness, justifying the vicious circle of theft.

Afterall, no one sees me: and it leaves its detrimental mark, it is another action of Untrustability, for example, littering.

He who does not suffer, does not win; no pain, no gain represents the culture of high or medium Trustability.

He who does not work, let him not eat it is a phrase from the Bible that is lived in the Jewish culture, which also represents the culture of high or medium Trustability, in a natural and obligatory way.

CHAPTER II - MODEL TO BUILD TRUST HO

He who does not live to serve, does not serve to live: a phrase attributed to Rabindranath Tagore, shows that correspondence between giving and receiving, like the oriental yin and yang, which encloses the concept of life. Life is movement, it arises from the continuous interaction between 2 poles, just as electricity is originated by the exchange of the positive pole of charge, with the negative one; so it happens with the 2 poles of life, one, living for oneself, and the other, living for others, where both are necessary to give life.

God helping God and the gavel giving: a phrase that shows that, although you depend on the Almighty, there are aspects of life that depend only on you. Only you and your will, your effort and your learning. Your turn. It is necessary to hit him hard with the Gavel.

It is imperative that in the 21st century it is seriously put on the table of society and of all countries to put an end to corruption that harms everyone.

Social concern about corruption should be seen as an opportunity to work seriously on increasing Trustability and honest and competent collaboration.

I remember, when I traveled to Japan, how the travel agency worked together with the hotels, in such a way that visitors' luggage, arrival and departure times, were handled by both and between the different hotels, with a magnificent voluntary coordination between them, taking work and inconvenience away from the traveler. This is achieved with the *Quality Model*, not because there is a central law and a central agency depending on the government, but by education in a *Model to Build Trust*. We have everything open to make it possible in other companies.

4. LEVELS OF TRUST

The idea is to prepare people to become experts in trustability assessment, both for individuals and companies.

This section is dedicated to them, to train them and give them bases and tools for the measurement of Trustability, using each factor of the *Model,* and then, a weighting to reach global results of Trustability, which give a diagnosis of where to work to increase Trustability.

Scale to establish degrees of Trustability and criteria to define each degree and its rationale:

- 0 TO 5 POSITIVES ABOVE ZERO.
- 0 TO NEGATIVE 5 BELOW ZERO.

It has to do with results. Results in the different times, events or situations that arise. Successful and unsuccessful results.

Generally, there is a high correlation between high mastery of the craft, i.e., the degree of depth achieved (already discussed in Section II.2 of the *Model to Build Trust HO.*) and the high level of results in the different Trustability assessments. It is about creating the habit of being Trustworthy.

We are going to establish and qualify certain Trustability Grades, in order to embark on the journey to improve Trustability itself.

- The first rule is to establish a purpose for trustability measurement that is precisely for *improvement*, in a collaborative and transparent manner, and never for destructive criticism.
- The second rule is to define in which field, trade, role, or specialty, Trustability is to be rated.

- The third rule is to define the scope of persons or sets of persons (group or department) to be rated.
- The fourth rule is to define the qualifiers: clients, users, qualified representative of the public, judge, *coach*.
- The fifth rule is to establish a *Time Framework*, i.e., a time horizon in the past, covering the rating and a rating period, going forward.

The extremes of the scale are easier to define.

The **+5** is for the greatest exponents recognized in the World, in that specialty, trade or role.

The **-5** is for people also recognized who are probably in jail or already dead but are condemned by society and are a worldwide example of NOT Trustworthy, in a certain trade or role. Let's say, Hitler, Stalin, and Lenin, who were already judged by history in their role as political leaders. Coincidentally, one of them, at one end of the insensitive and bloodthirsty right wing; the other two, at one end of the left wing, allegedly preaching equality, but being murderous.

The **+4, +3, +2, +1,** is for the following, in this order:

+4   Expert and Master of that trade or field, already recognized or certified.

+3   Advanced person, with many Practice Flight Hours and good results in their trade or role, who already does it naturally and has applied it in different places, locations, states, or different groups in countries.

+2   A person who is in the second level, starting to climb the steepest part of the learning curve, the one of greater difficulties, on the one hand, but of the satisfactions and results of personal stretching to reach greater goals in their field, as well as of recognition from others, on the other hand.

+1 A person who declares that they are a beginner, but who has already passed the probationary period to demonstrate willingness, vocation, commitment, and potential for further improvement.

0 Zero is the line that separates between being straight and being *crooked*; between being respectful of the laws, good customs and evading them, being a criminal and causing harm to others; between living with attachment to the objective truth and living in the continuous lie. At zero, there are infants and children, before the use of reason or people with a severe cognitive disability that affects consciousness.

-1 A person who already has a history of being unreliable, due to known and verifiable events, but who has an important reason not to become negative again, has the good intention and purpose to improve in the next 12 months, subject to verification.

-2 A person who has a history of being untrustworthy in higher degrees of deviation in the trade in question. There are doubts as to whether there are compelling reasons to be able to drastically improve its Trustability.

-3 A person who has a history of being untrustworthy in higher degrees of deviation in the trade at issue. In addition, they have not been convinced of their decision to improve their Trustability.

-4 A person who has demonstrated a lack of trustworthiness in serious cases, who has hurt society and shows no remorse, but rather shows a sense of not caring, or a sense of contempt for the profession, the clients, and users.

The journey to become more Trustworthy can start at **-1**, perhaps **-2,** when there is a lot of willingness, training and control of the improvement surrounding and controlling it and work its way up to **+5.**

One who is untrustworthy in their main occupation, or one who has an occupation that is of an untrustworthy nature, is very likely to be untrustworthy in their personal life.

The trades, specialties, or roles in which a person is qualified, should be some of personal life and others of work life.

There are 3 very important types of personal life:

1. Father, mother, son, daughter.
2. Citizen.
3. A non-working task.

There are 3 very important types of work life:

1. That of the profession itself as a trade.
2. That of your work, as a professional in what you do.
3. That of the company and/or department in which you work.

Of the Companies:

1. Manufacturing companies.
2. Commercial companies.
3. Construction companies.
4. Banks and financial businesses.
5. Of services.

6. Public service.

7. From government entities.

It is possible that this degree of Trustability may seem very complex and invasive, but the truth is that it can be implicit or explicit. If it is not explicit, be sure that your clients, bosses, children, partner, neighbors, rate without writing it down and you have their implicit rating.

That is why doing exercises, either internal, with oneself or open, are very convenient. Only what is measured can be improved. Remember that sportsmen, musicians, concert performers, doctors, pilots, operators of well-managed production plants, CEOs of well-managed companies, are always rated and evaluated, whether in each day, week, month, or in each transcendent event and the historical trend they lead, and it is better to feel it openly and formally objective, than underwater, in the opaque and subjective, without saying it, using it in a manipulative way.

It is urgent to do what is necessary to establish trustworthy performance measures in the political and public administration areas, since they have suffered from having this type of 21st century administration.

5. **CHAIN OF LINKS TO BE COVERED, IN ORDER TO BE A TRUSTWORTHY ORGANIZATION**
    1. Commitment and Trustability Profile of its leaders.
    2. Definition of Organizational Structure, Organizational and Management Policies.
    3. Client Orientation.
    4. Orientation to the people working in the company.
    5. Quality Control and Testing.
    6. Process Control and Certifications.
    7. Provider Relations.
    8. Results and Values.
    9. Audit.
    10. Corporate Image.

6. **ORGANIZATION TO INCREASE THE COMPANY'S TRUST**

In *Section II.2 of* this *Chapter*, all the functional concepts that it is advisable to adopt and implement for the execution of activities in a company, institution, or organization to be trustworthy were specified: *Model to Build Trust HO*.

These concepts can also be focused on trades, service o government institutions. I make a synthesis, as a *check list*, to give guidance on how to organize to be able to implement the *Model to Build Trust HO*.

1. That the leader takes the banner of being Trusted and promotes it officially, communicating it, both

institutionally and personally, above all, setting an example.

2. To have a platform of readings and forums to raise awareness and learn about Trustability, the whys and wherefores and its benefits.

3. To have a person or a department (if the company is large), responsible for promoting, developing, and conducting, by means of a specific plan, the different steps to be taken to implement the *Model to Build Trust HO*.

4. The minimum recommended modules to implement the *Model to Build Trust HO* are the following:

   4.1. Improved client satisfaction.

   4.2. Measurement and improvement of trustability in products and services.

   4.3. Detection of areas of opportunity and improvement of process trustability.

   4.4. Trustability Assurance of suppliers and inputs.

   4.5. Policies and Audit of Management Policies and Internal Control, including Control of Conflicts of Interest.

   4.6. Training and development of Talent in the Model to Build Trust HO and in the trade itself *(hard skills)*.

   4.7. Ongoing communication, recognition of Trustability achievements and lessons learned forums.

   4.8. Training of leaders with the attributes of the *Model to Build Trust HO*.

4.9. Contests, prizes, and motivation for High Trustability, extending the promotion to families, to spread the results of Trustability.

4.10. Implementation of Collaborative Models of human integration and integration to the company.

4.11. Evaluation, selection, and promotion of people who contribute highly to Trustability.

4.12. Results and evaluation of the cost-effectiveness and benefits of the *Model to Build Trust HO*.

CHAPTER III
TRUST PURPOSES

The purpose of Trustability is to have an impact on joint wellbeing and, if possible, to be sustainable over time, wellbeing, and progress.

1- WELLBEING

Trustability is a way of being of people who, together with their organizations and their communication and control systems, execute work or activities aimed at higher purposes. This is the means to have valuable satisfactions for oneself and, above all, for others, to whom they are useful and necessary.

I mentioned in previous chapters that it is about achieving Trustability in cases of human interactions, where goods and resources are exchanged with the intention of generating a useful and necessary additional value that was not possessed.

These useful and necessary satisfiers can be, at the same time, deficient, bad, regular, good, safe, unsafe, doubtful, or uncertain; Trustability is in charge of taking care of what is necessary to make them safe and Trustworthy for human wellbeing, communicating the truth and protecting the client and the user in their physical integrity, instructing, and informing appropriately the scope of that good, product or service.

This way of being generates trust in the society you serve. In other words, it is an activity's distinguishing feature, an adjective: to be trustworthy in its results or deliverables, and that confidence is earned by providing measurable and verifiable results in the perception of others.

Measurable rational evidence, on the one hand, and human warmth, kindness in service, on the other hand, are necessary to achieve that perception of others, which is biunivocal, ethical, honest, and effective, fulfilled, and measurable in what can be measured, tangible and helpful on the human side.

Being trustworthy directly includes thinking of others, i.e. the client and the user; seeking their satisfaction, safety, and integrity. This is demonstrated in the deliverable (product or service) and in the chain of human interactions that are behind this product, service, people, etc. Trustworthy throughout the chain, all the way to the end client and the user.

Trustability is a companion of the person and methodology used to provide a service, product, or human interaction. To provide confidence is that there are real intentions to cause a benefit to the wellbeing, avoiding doing harm.

Wellbeing is to be satisfied and in good health; it is to have peace, harmony, balance and, if possible, to feel fulfilled and happy.

According to Maslow's pyramid of human needs, when basic needs, known as physiological needs, such as health, food, housing, and clothing, are satisfied, other higher aspirations arise, which have to do with satisfying desires for personal fulfillment and altruistic goals of service to others.

You cannot be a trustworthy person, organization, or company if you deliberately and maliciously cause something contrary to wellbeing. There is no such thing as being Trustworthy in delivering a service or product that causes harm to the wellbeing of others or to oneself: either you are

Trustworthy and cause benefit, or you are not Trustworthy because you cause harm.

If possible, it should be ensured that the satisfier is sustainable over time or, in other words, that the satisfier can be renewed in some way, meets needs and is valuable in the future.

This means that the Trustworthy person, as a provider, thinks about the present and the future of their clients, since they are empathetic with them in order to achieve their wellbeing.

Now, to be Trustworthy, from the client's point of view, means that the provider's good production will be stimulated, fulfilling the payment agreements. In addition, it is important, as a client, to communicate to the provider your evaluation of the product or service, the impact on satisfaction and recommendations to increase Trustability.

It must be said that, in addition, there are many possible satisfiers to improve wellbeing, standard of living and quality of life. The possibility of obtaining them arises from the exchange of valuable information among the participants.

If we want to generate wellbeing, we must start by seeking the wellbeing of ourselves, of our closest neighbors and then the wellbeing of other people around us. Satisfying these 3 levels of social outreach is a great goal.

2- SELF-ESTEEM AND WELLBEING

In *Chapter I, Item 2:* we said, about truth motivation, that the body detects when there is an incongruence and lack of truth between your intention, your core belief, your thoughts, your desires, your decisions, your verbal communication, your *body language,* and your actions. What you get when there is high incongruence and deviations from the truth is not wellbeing. The internal tension that you cause yourself can only generate discomfort, illness and, in severe cases, physical, mental, emotional disabilities or death. So, in the matter of being Trustworthy, you yourself are the first subject of wellbeing.

We said in previous paragraphs, when defining *Wellbeing* that, according to Maslow's pyramid of needs, there are higher internal satisfiers that have to do with your personal fulfillment. That is, personal fulfillment is the cause of personal wellbeing, healthy and generator of positive energy to live and progress.

To achieve personal fulfillment, you start by first being self-sufficient, both in material and non-material resources, and then being in a position to be able to give something valuable that you already have, and that is also valuable to your neighbor.

Having said that, we can assure you that Trustability directly impacts your wellbeing in 3 very powerful ways:

1. You avoid diseases by being congruent.
2. You satisfy a need of your own, which results in an increase in your personal fulfillment and better service to others.
3. You generate reciprocity; by giving a benefit to others, you also benefit yourself. The good you provide is returned to you multiplied.

3- THE WELLBEING OF OTHERS

The only thing that justifies the establishment of a business, job, service, government, organization, or family is that it has a legitimate desire to affect the wellbeing of others and of the members or social groups involved.

Therefore, when harm is done to others, the raison d'être of business, work, service, government, organization, and family is lost. Because, when a harm is done to others, motivated to achieve one's own benefit, the need for and importance of controlling Conflicts of Interest is denoted.

4- WELLBEING - TRUST BINOMIAL

Three characteristics of the product or service must be distinguished: *the Good*, in terms of the satisfaction or wellbeing it produces for the customer:

1. **Trustability in the Use of** the Good, which refers to what Americans call: *customization*, which implies adapting the product to the user as much as possible; that is, customizing the product to the weight, height, age, or physical dimensions of the client, for example.

2. The **Structural Trustability** of the Good, its constitution or, in other words, the properties of that GOOD; its structure, so that it lasts over time and that includes its ease of repair or maintenance.

3. **Trustability in the processes** involved in producing and supplying the Good, by which it was produced or manufactured and delivered. Let's call it Trustability in the quality of its origin, production, or manufacture.

If we make a graph where on the horizontal axis of the X, we measure the *Low, Medium* or *High Wellbeing,* and on the Y axis, we measure the Trustability in the use, we can say that it is the equivalent to sustainability of that wellbeing.

We have the following:

5- WELLBEING - USE BINOMIAL

WELLBEING - USE BINOMIAL		
A lot of Wellbeing and Very Appropriate Use	⟶	Health and Trustability
A lot of Wellbeing and Inadequate Use	⟶	Health, Distrust and Discomfort
Low Wellbeing and Highly Adequate Use	⟶	Discomfort and Comfort
Poor Wellbeing and Inadequate Use	⟶	Discomfort, Distrust and Uneasiness

6- USE-QUALITY BINOMIAL IN THE STRUCTURE OF THE GOOD

USE-QUALITY BINOMIAL IN THE STRUCTURE OF THE GOOD		
Good Suitability and Structure	→	Excellence and Trustability
Good Suitability and Poor Structure	→	Temporary Satisfaction
Poor Suitability and Good Structure	→	Dissatisfaction
Poor Suitability and Poor Structure	→	Dissatisfaction and Distrust

7- USE-QUALITY BINOMIAL IN THE MANUFACTURING PROCESSES OF THE PRODUCT

USE-QUALITY BINOMIAL IN THE MANUFACTURING PROCESSES OF THE PRODUCT		
Good Suitability and Good Processes	→	Excellence
Good Suitability and Poor Processes	→	Temporary Satisfaction and Distrust
Poor Suitability and Good Processes	→	Dissatisfaction
Inadequate Suitability and Deficient Processes	→	Dissatisfaction and Distrust

8- WELLBEING - TRUST

WELLBEING - TRUST		
High Wellbeing and High Trustability	⟶	Trustworthy and Permanent High Well-Being
High Wellbeing and Low Trustability	⟶	Temporary Satisfaction and Distrust
Low Wellbeing and High Trustability	⟶	Dissatisfaction and Safety
Low Wellbeing and Low Trustability	⟶	High Dissatisfaction and High Distrust

The Wellbeing-Trustability Binomial can be exemplified by a well-known asset: a house.

- *High Wellbeing and High Trustability* can be a very well-built house, in a safe place and that does not lose value, but on the contrary, gains it day by day (progress and satisfaction).

- *Low Wellbeing* and *Low Trustability*, it can be a wooden shack with a roof made of waste sheets, located in a very insecure place, with continuous threats, which produces possible diseases and, in addition, the risk of losing your life (scarce resources).

- *High Wellbeing* and *Low Trustability, it* can be a well-built house, with all the amenities, next to a river, which when it overflows, can quickly demolish, and wash away the house (wealth without livelihood).

- *Low Wellbeing* and *High Trustability*, it is a shaky hut in a very safe place, both favorable climate and a surrounding that protects you in itself (low resources and high security).

Being Trustworthy is pretty close to giving you security.

Trustability always seeks your good, your wellbeing and that of others.

Trustability is giving you physical, intellectual, and emotional protection.

The former, physical protection is more tangible and measurable than intellectual and emotional protection, but the latter are also of vital importance for life and wellbeing.

To be trustworthy is to communicate honestly the scope of the good, its possible consequences on wellbeing and, in addition, to comply with what has been agreed. Each case must be judged on its own merits depending on the circumstances and resources available.

According to the Binomial of Wellbeing-Trustability, any of the 4 cases of the houses shown could be Trustworthy if it is honestly communicated what each one means, it is warned of its possible consequences and, based on this information, the client decides to buy it. In other words, one can be trustworthy if one proceeds from the truth, respecting the freedom and will of others, controlling possible personal conflicts of interest.

When what you deliver as a provider exceeds your client's expectations, you get a good mark for your Trustability, you get to position yourself as a trustworthy person to others.

When what you deliver as a provider does not meet your client's expectations, then what you get is a negative mark for your Trustability. Is it because your client's expectations were too high and unfounded, but your product or service you delivered is the one actually offered? Is it because what was offered was not delivered, or was delivered, but below specifications? Both cases lose Trustability, but the second case is worse. This consideration and weighting are important only in explanatory terms for yourself, since, in both cases, it is necessary to resort to the client to reach new agreements that facilitate a material and emotional solution.

The example of houses is very applicable to many life circumstances that are very representative of the Wellbeing-Trustability Binomial. Below is an illustration in the circumstances of sailing at sea.

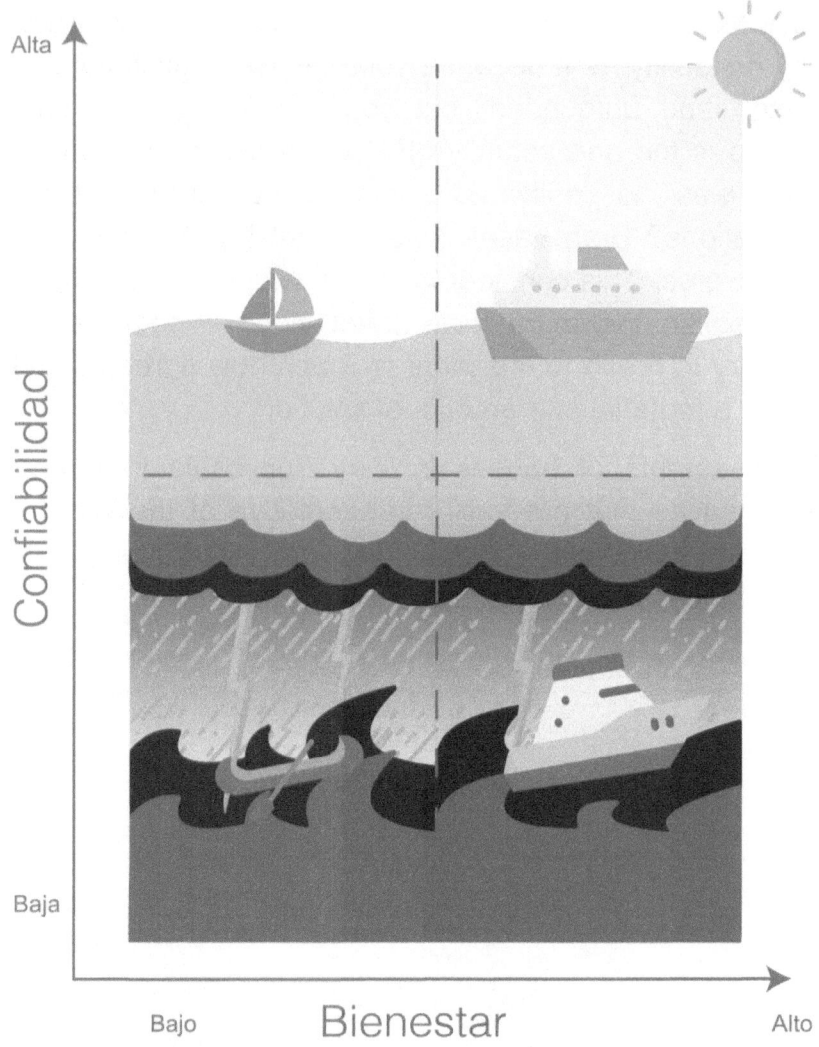

When what you deliver as a provider is exactly what the client expects and matches what is actually offered, you have given a trustworthy and fair deal.

On the other hand, if we talk about *Subsidiary Value of the good*, or *subsidized value*, it is when you offer the good below market value, either because of its suitability for use or because of its durability and warranty characteristics, or because of its trustworthy manufacturing processes.

An example of this is when you help: you give, provide, or support your neighbor in a temporary or partial way, but in a Trustworthy way, as part of teaching the way to fish for oneself and to become self-sufficient. It is when you have the trustworthy intention that your neighbor learns something to subsist, to be better, and thus, to give them not only some resources, but also an education or guidance that will help them to be self-sufficient in the future.

Now, we can speak of *Solidarity Value of Good*, when you give something for free for charitable or philanthropic reasons.

To be in solidarity with your neighbor is when you give, provide, or support with the idea of doing so unconditionally. In cases of children, elderly, sick or disabled people, the concept of solidarity is very much applied.

We have the example of Mother Teresa of Calcutta; in politics, the cases of Martin Luther King, Nelson Mandela, Gandhi, Abraham Lincoln; what they gave was of great solidarity value, of High Trustability and High Wellbeing.

For the experts and experts in Trustability assessment, we will develop the Trustability measurements in relation to wellbeing, as follows, based on the *20 Factors* of the *Model to Build Trust HO*:

- Private Companies.
- People.
- Schools.
- Public Entities (Municipalities, States, Federation).
- Public Companies.
- Decentralized organizations.
- Social organizations.

The idea is to measure the wellbeing factors and to measure the Trustability factors; evaluate them by experts and weight them to obtain a final, comparative rating in the sector.

In Wellbeing: Satisfaction, comfort, speed, personal taste, health.

In Trustability: suitability for customized use, safety, warranty, maintenance, spare parts, response time, added value.

Examples of High Excellence and High Trustability:

- Parents with their children throughout their lives; children with a lot of wellbeing, communication, and strong dependence, first, as minors, and then, independence as adults. In the end, that's when they value both worlds: being treated as a child and being treated as more responsible and independent.
- Educational institutions that, over time, have been and continue to be successful and beloved, such as the Tecnológico de Monterrey, for example.

- Hospitals that have existed for a long time and continue to be recognized and admired, such as the Christus Muguerza Hospital in Monterey and the ABC Hospital *in* Mexico City.

There are examples of High Wellbeing and High Trustability among many sectors of companies and institutions, of many products and services, of greater or lesser social impact; some Highly Trustworthy and others not so much.

What I propose is that we distinguish them by evaluating and recognizing their impact, both in terms of wellbeing and trustability.

If we do so, we will promote a culture of High Wellbeing and High Trustability, which is in everyone's best interest. Those it does not favor are the *lazy ones* and those who dedicate themselves to take the short path of lies and deceit to achieve their personal desires and benefits, which harm others.

There are many entities that have proven, for a long time, their worth in the use of their products, services and, above all, in their Trustability, that have an honest history of service and high user satisfaction to back them up.

I have a few companies in mind: Caterpillar, Rolex, Sony, Apple, Amazon, HEB, BOEING, General Motors, Disney; many families that have been educating several generations well, in producing wellbeing to others, being trustworthy, and that can serve as references.

In the history of companies, statistically speaking, there is much difficulty in the permanence of companies when changing generations; when the founder is passed on to the next generation, there is much mortality of companies; when it manages to transcend to the second generation, there is much difficulty for it to remain in the third generation. In the transfer of generations, it is recognized in a colloquial way, as a working-visionary father, a working son, and a living grandson.

Therefore, some of the companies mentioned in High Trustability deserve double recognition for their Trustability and also for their culture of making permanence possible.

Who are we proud of in our society for producing High Wellbeing with High Trustability?

Some companies could give us many pleasant surprises if we evaluate and discover how they work for the good of others, producing wellbeing with High Trustability.

First, we must recognize the positive, ignite enthusiasm, and then undertake solutions to overcome the positive, improve the mediocre and have the strength to correct the negative.

Every company, institution and family must be measured in this context of confidently producing wellbeing. Universities should promote careers as facilitators of wellbeing and trustability improvement.

Undermining the durability of Trust is very serious, since trust takes time to build, it comes as a result of *many good ones*, but is lost very quickly, with two or three bad ones.

When an entire sector has not earned the recognition of High Trustability, it can be assumed that the entire country in that sector is deficient.

Organisms could be created to promote the culture of Wellbeing and Trustability by distinguishing the good ones; fines could also be applied to the bad ones, but only when you already have the recognition of a Moral Authority, when you have already earned the trust of your users.

Wellbeing and Trustability is the way, there is no other way. Do not turn it over. Do not use *lazy road cutters* that are not sustainable.

The *Model to Build Trust HO* aims to stimulate the culture of Wellbeing and Trustability; not only to stimulate and create awareness, that would not be enough, but to provide the solution for those who want it. Provide the means, methods, advice, courses, *coaching*, classes, recognition.

The current era needs it, because we come from an era where children were badly educated to be *lazy* and not to be concerned about being trustworthy, with all the burden that this entails, for the sake that *there is only one life and you have to spend it as best as possible*, understanding that the best possible is to do as little as possible for others and live only for yourself.

The coming generation, *post-millennials*, by human nature, are aware of this, and there is a huge potential to reverse these Untrustworthy trends, for High Trustability trends, if we dedicate ourselves to it.

We join Jordan Peterson, a Canadian psychologist, who preaches the urgent reversal of these trends, and who holds the premise that: *greater responsibility, starting at a younger age, builds more confident and happier people*.

EPILOGUE

WELL-BEING, HAPPINESS AND FULFILLMENT

The path of seeking sustainable well-being for oneself and others, with Trustability, is a sure way to achieve Wellbeing, Happiness and Fulfillment.

1- WHY DID YOU COME INTO THE WORLD?

THESIS OF THE BOOK:

Why did you come into the world?

A) To get your immediate pleasure every time.

B) To learn from nature and natural phenomena.

C) To coexist with other humans with good results.

D) To know creation and transcend together with that creation.

E) The best solution would be to have a bad time, sacrifice oneself and wait to die.

What your *superficial self* says is, to get your pleasure, this is item A; what your *true self* or *deep self* says, is B, C and D; and what a *victimized self* says, I mean, those who consider themselves victims of everything, is E.

The thesis of this book is to achieve Happiness and Fulfillment.

Happiness and Fulfillment is broader, as it includes the 3 aspects of life, B, C and D.

2- TRUST PATH

The path of seeking sustainable wellbeing for oneself and others, with Trustability, is a sure way to achieve happiness and fulfillment, referring to a *true self* 's belief in seeking B, C and D.

Neither of the 2 extremes, neither A nor E, belong to the path of seeking sustainable wellbeing, for oneself and others, in a Trustworthy manner.

You are composed of Mind, Body and Spirit. To seek Happiness and Fullness of life means that Mind, Body and Spirit are in harmony, conjugation and orientation towards truth, peace, and freedom. This orientation is achieved through a well-balanced self-development that is reflected in your being, knowing, doing, and having.

If you have another thesis of life, where you do not believe that the search for truth, peace and responsible freedom are the paths to pursue with the resources you have, which are your Mind, Body and Spirit, then there will be no efficient communication between this book and you.

This is because the chain of links of intentions, beliefs, attitudes, emotions, competencies, and actions, with results, must have a support and a conjugation around higher values.

If you believe in these higher values of truth, peace, and freedom, with their corresponding complexities and ambiguities, then the path of Happiness and Fulfillment is worth embarking on.

In this path of Happiness and Fulfillment, the route of seeking the sustainable wellbeing of oneself and others, with Trustability, is recommended and safe.

The road with this route is complex and difficult, but full of satisfactions.

It is a continuous struggle between you and your circumstances, between your *superficial self* and your deeper *true self* .

We are able to go by what the *self* says, and we are able to go where the *true self* says. It is a matter of choice, as there is the freedom to choose.

If you choose the belief of being free, with responsibility for your actions, you are on your way to being a Trustworthy person; it is one of the consequences. If you choose the belief of being a dependent slave to others, the consequence is that you are not responsible and, therefore, Untrustworthy.

The mind sometimes thinks that the world is a certain way: *the way you want it to be*; but the body truly reflects to you whether that belief is objectively true or not. The connection of body and mind with spirit allows you to point out the realities of life, although sometimes your desires get in the way.

Belief in a spiritual life is more objective than beliefs that there is no more than the tangible, the mass, the particles that can be seen and touched. The belief that the intangible precedes the tangible is more objective than believing that the tangible is given by itself. A thought that is intangible generates tangible substances such as hormones, for example. A positive thought generates a certain type of substance, and a negative thought generates another type of substance in our body.

Trial and error, learning from your own or others' experiences, experimenting with the flesh of others and our ancestors, give you a good indication of which results are best.

Observe the results you have on your life and happiness if you choose certain thoughts that you develop and grow healthy; observe the results you have on your happiness if you choose to adopt negative and destructive thoughts of your body.

At the end of the day, you will know people by their outcomes, which are precisely their results. Outcomes that help others are, precisely, the positive results of living with others, item C.

Wellbeing, Happiness and Fulfillment are sought-after outcomes.

3- WELLBEING

Wellbeing refers to the fact that you are in good health, with energy to be able to carry out the actions you want to do in your life.

4- HAPPINESS

Happiness refers to being at peace and with inner satisfaction with your positive emotions and, generally, in favorable circumstances that cause you great satisfaction.

5- PLENITUDE

Fullness refers to the fact that every moment, every second, regardless of what is happening (circumstances around you), the internalization of what happens and your reaction to what happens is satisfactory, is harmonious, is understandable by you, is excellent, projects outcomes to others, projects light and good energy.

BIBLIOGRAPHY

Arizpe, J. F. (2012). *¿Cómo Ser Más Producivo y Feliz?* USA: Trafford.

Hawkins, D. R. (2004). *Power vs. Force: The Hidden Determinants of Human Behavior* USA: Hay House.

Jordan, M. (1994). *I Can't Accept Not Trying: Michael Jordan on the Pursuit of Excellence.* USA: Harper San Francisco.

Peterson, J. (2019*). 12 reglas para vivir: Un antídoto al caos.* Mexico: Planeta.

JORGE FARIAS ARIZPE

I was fortunate that, since I was very young, I liked many things in life, learning different subjects at school, living with friends, recreation, sports, parties of my extended family and good relationships with my parents, siblings, aunts, uncles, grandparents, cousins; in other words, I lived with people of all ages, adults, my own age and younger than me. I use the masculine but referring to both men and women.

On the one hand, I developed humanistic topics in psychology and history, on the other hand, in management, and on the other hand, in mathematics, engineering and science.

All these subjects were always accompanied by sports, being basketball, tennis, but also baseball, swimming, golf, soccer, bicycling, hiking, trekking, martial arts, horseback riding, motorcycling and tap.

In professional work I first developed some sales and sales management, then, all the specialty of Human Capital, Business Planning and Management, in addition to managing businesses and investments.

In the world of Human Capital, I started offering technical training to maintenance supervisors, and from there, to develop all specialties: Wage, Salary and Compensation Administration; Design of Organization Structures; Organizational Development; Executive Planning and Development; Total Quality; Labor Law Administration; Recruitment and Selection at all levels; Industrial Safety; Sports and Cultural Clubs for workers.

As specialties within consulting I developed Organizational Structure Design; Executive Planning and Development; Competitiveness based on Organization; Human Capital and Total Quality; Management Succession; Organizational Development; and Management Models based on Objectives and Accountability.

I now wish to develop the Trustability Specialty in companies as well as in institutions and individuals.

I had the privilege of sailing many seas, that is, in many different sectors of the world of work and economy, being the most valuable thing to learn from so many wonderful people, working.

- From chemical, petrochemical, and plastics companies:

    CYDSA, Alfa, TUK, Stabilit, Vitro.

- From the metal-mechanical, automotive, and capital goods sectors:

    HYLSA, IMSA, GIS, CERREY General Motors, Grupo Hermes, Aceromex, Criotec, Mabe, Whilpool, Proeza, Partes de Turbinas OTM, among others.

- From the manufacturing sector of products for the construction industry:

    Cemex, Lamosa, Vitromex, Orion, Vitro, ADS Mexicana.

- Manufacturing of food and beverage consumer products:

    HERDEZ, Alen, Gamesa, Coca-Cola ARMA, Cuervo, Vitro, FEMSA, Villa de Patos, INFRA, Montana Muebles, Hotel Sheraton, Bebidas Garciarce.

- Textile Manufacturing:

    Bamex, Plasticel, DASA, ARMA.

- Banking and Financial Services:

    Bancomer, Probursa, Grupo Financiero Interacciones, Laredo NATIONAL BANK.

- Commercial, Services and Retail:

    Comercial Mexicana, Valores Corporativos, Icon, SEVEN Eleven, FEMSA, Grupo Ley, Aeromexico, Agencias de autos Chevrolet, Mercedes Benz, Motocicletas y Equipos, EMWA.

- Construction:

    Internacional de Inversiones, NEST, Dynamica, Abitat, Recsa, Grupo HERMES, Carza, Desarrollos GOSA.

- Telecommunications:

    Telcel, Axtel.

- Education:

    ITESM, UERRE, UNID, Talisis, EDEC.

- Health:

    Christus Muguerza Hospital, Hospitaria, Alivio Capital.

- Insurance:

    GNP, AER.

- Social institutions and foundations:

    Coparmex, CPNL, ANTAD, INFONAVIT, Comunidar, ANSPAC, USEM, LMB.

As an author, I have had the pleasure of contributing the following publications:

- Dirección de Capital Humano: Énfasis en Perfilamiento y Desarrollo (2006).
- Sé Consciente de tu Ser: Inteligencia Espiritual (2007).

- Dirección de Capital Humano (Trillas, 2011).
- Cómo ser más productivo y feliz (2012).
- El Reto de México: Aumentar la Confiabilidad (2021).

In summary:
- 4 years as a child.
- 11 years as a student with the Marist brothers.
- 5 years of IMA professional career at Tecnológico de Monterrey.
- 20 years in CYDSA.
- 33 years in MGT.
- 4 children.
- 2 sons-in-law.
- 1 daughter-in-law.
- 12 grandchildren.
- 6 siblings with their partners.
- My wife María Esther.
- 3 stepchildren with their partners.
- And many friends, clients, godchildren and nieces and nephews.

Thank God for the privilege of learning from so many valuable people.

www.ingramcontent.com/pod-product-compliance
Lightning Source LLC
Chambersburg PA
CBHW031615210526
45464CB00004B/1592